Sons of a Good Keen Man

Sons of a Good Keen Man

Life in the shadow of Barry Crump

The Crump Brothers

PENGUIN BOOKS

PENGUIN

UK | USA | Canada | Ireland | Australia
India | New Zealand | South Africa | China

Penguin is an imprint of the Penguin Random House group of companies, whose addresses can be found at global.penguinrandomhouse.com.

First published by Penguin Random House New Zealand, 2022

10 9 8 7 6 5 4 3 2 1

Design by Carla Sy © Penguin Random House New Zealand
Front cover photograph courtesy Ans Westra
Back cover photograph courtesy *New Zealand Herald* archive
Extract on pages 16 and 19 reproduced from Colin Crump, *In Endless Fear: A True Story*, Penguin, 2002, with kind permission of the Colin Crump estate
Prepress by Soar Communications Group
Printed and bound in Australia by Griffin Press, an Accredited ISO AS/NZS 14001 Environmental Management Systems Printer

A catalogue record for this book is available from the National Library of New Zealand.

ISBN 978-1-76104-718-3
eISBN 978-1-76104-719-0

penguin.co.nz

Contents

Barry at the family home
on Astley Avenue.

Introduction

One of the things that ties us together, we sons of Barry Crump - the fabled Good Keen Man - is that we all do our best not to think about him. Each of us has often wished we were born into someone else's family and legacy. But we weren't. And we've had to stand up and face our lot in life.

Barry could be funny, entertaining, charming, and wonderful company; he was, of course, a gifted storyteller and talented writer.

He could also be a violent, sadistic coward; a selfish, obnoxious arsehole who could be extremely cruel to animals and people who got too close to him.

Barry had six children, all boys. Not one of us were planned or wanted by him. We are simply the product of sex. That's our reality.

It's also the reality for many others. And we are certainly not the only family to have suffered abandonment or violence. We are all from broken homes, and have possibly seen much more than we should have, as is the case for many people out there. Our family just happened to live out our dysfunction in view of the public, and much was recorded for all to see.

As we get to know our parents, we get to know ourselves. When I began to find out about the details of Barry's own horrendous upbringing, it opened my eyes to why he could not be a father to us. Having now read all of my brothers' stories, I can see we are all quite different people, who have lived different lives, but we share one unique and undeniable thing that somehow binds us. He still left his mark, the good and the bad - and we have had to live with both.

Barry has been gone for more than twenty-five years now, but he still looms large, as you will see in the pages that follow.

The story behind this book begins more than a decade ago, when Jeremy Sherlock, a non-fiction publisher for Penguin, got in touch. He told me that he believed a book told by the children of Barry Crump would be of interest to many, and that it would make for a great read. I wasn't so sure myself.

For some reason, Jeremy couldn't or wouldn't let it be. The years passed and he pitched the idea to me again, with the same belief and conviction. While I was keener this time around, the decision wasn't mine to make alone.

I asked my brothers if they would like to be involved in such a project - and they all very quickly got back to me with an emphatic yes. They wanted to tell their story, to be heard. I imagine my brothers, like me, have grown up deep in the shadow of our well-known father with little or no voice of their own.

And so our stories are not simply *told by* the sons of Barry Crump, but have been *written by* us. They are a very honest and real account of what our childhood and adult life has been like.

I had more time with Barry than my brothers did, which seems a bit unfair - but that's just how it played out. Given this, and with me being one of the oldest, I arguably lead proceedings, though we share the storytelling, with my brothers all contributing fascinating reflections and anecdotes, many of which were new to me. These are largely - but not always - presented in chronological order.

As I say, our book relays each brother's experience, how we have navigated our way through life, and where we are now - in our own words. This has been a difficult but ultimately rewarding process; we each lived largely separate lives and knew Barry in very different ways. The stories we share reflect our fragmented memories but, we hope, cohere into a powerful whole for the reader.

As a guide to the book, us and our respective stories, brief introductions are likely required:

- **IVAN CRUMP:** born 1958, son of Tina, now based in the Hokianga
- **MARTIN CRUMP:** born 1959, son of Tina, now based in West Auckland
- **STEPHEN LINDLEY:** born 1960, son of Jean, now based in Wellington
- **HARRY WATSON:** born 1965, son of Jean, now based in Masterton
- **ERIK WESTRA:** born 1965, son of Ans, now based in Rotorua
- **LYALL CRUMP:** born 1970, son of Vanda, now based in Ohakune

Naturally, our mums and families feature prominently throughout our stories. It's worth recording that Barry was married five times, as follows: to Tina Anso (1957), Fleur Adcock (1962), Vanda Hill (1969), Robin Hughes (1979) and Maggie Nicholson (1993).

At the end of the day, what sets this book apart from all other accounts of Barry's life is that it is not about him. It is about us. Barry's an obvious presence - except for when he's absent - and might be seen in a new light through the lens of our lives.

I hope that writing and sharing our stories will help heal what needs healing, forgive what needs forgiving, and enable us to live our own lives as best we can.

Martin Crump, August 2022

Prologue

Dear Barry,

Just a note to say I didn't overall enjoy the shadow you cast over me and mine. Especially as everyone I met thought you were so wonderful. Some people may have found you immensely attractive but what were you to me?

To me, you were always distant. Any personal conversations were like pulling teeth. It was difficult having you be so well known. Most people had ideas that didn't go with my own experiences at all.

You would turn into a most dangerous animal over fuck all. This was not appreciated. You pulling a gun on your brother Bill when he came to see you - once again, not fucking appreciated.

I say all of this in a most forgiving way, as I too am a weak and pathetic bastard - this we share.

When you were dying, you were coma'd out and I remember thinking that all of your drug-taking, womanising and fame were nothing compared to the trip you were about to take.

I do admire you in many ways, but your absence really fucking hurt and certainly coloured my life. I wouldn't have minded being beaten up as a child if that was the price to pay to have you around. It might have been better if you were dead my whole life, for my sake.

Your son,
Ivan

Barry gone bush, early 1960s.

1.

The Making of a Man

Barry's early years

'He was called dopey so often by his father that he started to believe it.'

MARTIN Two weeks after Barry died, we heard that his father, Wally, had also just passed away. On the day of Wally's funeral, my uncle Colin told me he'd pick me up, saying he had something to tell me, something I should know.

I got in his car. I noticed Colin was on a mission, determined, like something had changed in him. Something had. My eyes were about to be truly opened to what really went on in the Crump family home - what no one saw behind closed doors.

When we arrived at the funeral venue, Colin saw someone he recognised. He leaned across me and pointed out an older, white-haired man across the road from us.

'That's your great uncle John. See the person standing twenty feet away from him? Well, that's his son. They haven't spoken for twenty years and it's over absolutely nothing. They're just miserable sons of bitches,' Colin said, through clenched teeth.

I said nothing. I just listened.

We went inside to meet the preacher in charge of the day's proceedings.

Colin told him straight: 'I want no waffling on about how much of a great guy my father was. I want the absolute minimum said and get him in the ground, or I'll read this out.'

With that, he pulled a wad of paper out of his pocket. The

preacher did as Colin asked. I don't blame him. The ceremony was over very quickly.

On the way home, Colin told me what was on the paper in his pocket. I was shocked. Barry only ever said his father was a hard old man. I never knew the truth, not until this moment. He wasn't 'hard' - he was a monster.

And to think, for two years later in his life, I prepared so many meals for him. It would have been different if I had known the extent of things.

Some time later, I spoke to Barry's older brother, Uncle Bill, about his upbringing. He couldn't remember eight years of his childhood - he had completely blocked it out, it was that bad.

Barry caught the worst of the beatings. He was bashed so brutally once that he hid under the house for several days to recover, his sisters sneaking him food to help keep him alive. They were so worried about him.

He was called dopey so often by his father that he started to believe it.

My grandmother Lily, a deeply religious woman, was found in the wash house one day with a piece of her scalp lying on the floor.

Their life was hell at the hands of this monster. This, of course, was a time when hitting your children was allowed as a form of discipline. What about killing them?

Uncle Colin would go on to write the story of the Crump children's upbringing in his book *In Endless Fear* - it's a raw, discomforting account of their often brutal childhood, exemplified by the following brief but hideous excerpt:

> He had a length of milking machine hose in his
> hand and I watched in terror as once more he laid
> into my brother Barry with his merciless thrashing

Barry and his father, Wally
— aka the monster.

Barry (centre) with his brothers
Colin (left) and Bill.

> that just went on and on. Then he turned to me – they were really ferocious blows. The weapon he had chosen was, without doubt, the worst we had ever endured. I yelled, screamed, pleaded, cried, and of course, wet myself.
>
> We eventually crept back up to the house where Mum had a bath ready, and when we took off our clothes and she saw the vicious welts and bruises, she broke down and wept. We really were a hell of a mess, but even worse was the shouting and abuse that took place during the night because Mum was speaking up on our behalf, resulting in her getting slapped about too. More fears, more tears, followed by even more of both.

That book told me so much; it helped me understand my father better and made it so much easier to forgive his failings. It can't have been easy for Colin to write all this down, to live through it again. I hope it helped him in some way.

To my aunties Shirley and Carol, to my uncles Bill, Colin and Peter, to my father Barry, to my grandmother Lily – we now know what you went through. Let's hope no more children – or adults, for that matter – from this family have to endure what you had to.

I've spoken to my auntie Shirley about this time in her life – I can see her now as I write this, and it breaks my heart when I see the look on her face as she recalls the nightmare. Wally was the ripe old age of 87 when he died. That's not even fair.

IVAN The more information I've gleaned over the years, the more respect I have for Barry as a person. Anyone going through the type of childhood he had had to have been fucked up real bad, and he somehow rose above it. The years in the bush were the buffer, I expect.

Barry's father was a particularly vicious and ugly-minded man, and though I lay no claim to his particular form of excess, I do find it easy to behave violently.

'Anyone going through the type of childhood he had had to have been fucked up real bad, and he somehow rose above it.'

The story goes that the Crump children were sitting at the table having dinner. Barry accidentally spilled a cup of something on his eldest sister. Barry's father, Wally, nearly killed Barry for that. Really let him suffer. Barry lived under the house for three days, recovering. Carol, his sister, took what food she could to him. He survived.

Barry's old man would throw boiling water over a reluctant cow to get it to move when he was milking. His wife, Lily, told the kids that he had the devil in him. Lily was hospitalised from his cruelty and violence a few times. Barry found his mother knocked out in a pool of blood more than once.

One day, Carol stood up to Wally and he backed down. Typical bully and coward. My advice is, as much you're able, to always stand up to any behaviour resembling that sort of thing.

After talking with one of Barry's sisters about his upbringing, I have only respect for him being as good as he was. With such a history, I imagine he could have delivered a fair bit of what he got, for sure, if any of us had been in his care.

Lyall (left) and his brother Alan.

2.

Boys Will Be Boys

Our early years

‘Barry was an awesome dad to many children, just not his own.’

MARTIN There is something that has always bothered me, and this may well be the perfect place to put it right.

The number of Barry's children has been widely and incorrectly reported. Barry even got it wrong in his own autobiography! There, he says he has nine sons. He's included some of his stepsons, which is nice but not accurate and confuses everyone. So here it is once and for all. In his life, Barry fathered six children, all boys: Ivan, Martin, Stephen, Harry, Erik and Lyall. There, I feel better already.

Barry lived with and played a part in a number of other children's lives, but not his own. That was a responsibility he could not handle.

This was made clear to me only after his death, when his own horrendous and disturbing upbringing was revealed.

Barry and my mum would have eight marriages between them, which could appear messy to some, but for my brother Ivan and me, it was normal.

Mum had already lived a life before Barry came onto the scene. She was barely sixteen when she innocently and naively met and married a monster who was twenty years her senior. They would have two children together.

When the monster left Mum, he went on to marry Mum's

Barry and wife Tina, 1957.

sister, and they had seven children together. So now my cousins were brothers and sisters to my brother and sister. I wish you well figuring that lot out.

It's a shame my grandparents couldn't have protected Mum from that monster, but they did provide a home for her in Astley Avenue, New Lynn, in West Auckland, which they bought off the poet Rex Fairburn in the mid-1950s.

The house would go on to become a wonderful family home for generations, and is where my own children were born.

'Barry lived with and played a part in a number of other children's lives, but not his own. That was a responsibility he could not handle.'

My grandmother Ruby, all five feet of her, was a dynamo, a great provider and tireless worker. She bought the house at Astley Avenue; she also died in that house, in 1980, after a full and colourful life. We wouldn't have wanted it any other way.

Ruby's friends, who visited often, included the broadcaster Peter Sinclair. It was our large cane chair from home that he sat in when he hosted the very popular TV shows *C'mon* and *Happen Inn* on Saturday nights in the late 1960s.

She was also a good friend to writer Frank Sargeson, who incidentally wrote a short story about my grandfather Bill, titled 'The Hole that Jack Dug', because Bill was in the habit of digging holes all over the property - he just loved digging.

One day he dug a hole in the backyard so deep he couldn't get out of it. Mum heard him from the kitchen calling for her to help him get out.

My brothers and I once built a hut, a decent-sized one at that, then one day after school the hut was gone. Bill had dug a hole and buried it, but what was hard to believe is that he didn't pull it apart first - just buried it whole!

He was part Estonian - his father Martin had been in the Russian Tsar's navy. He jumped ship and made his way to New Zealand. Our house became the Communist Party headquarters for Auckland.

Mum had a job handing out theatre programmes at the Saint James, to help out with money at home. Her circle of friends included all sorts of characters: university, literary and artistic people who would come and go from Astley Avenue. Mum's parties were wild and alive with conversation, with an open-door policy. We once had someone come to stay for the night and end up staying a year.

It was in 1957 when Mum, with a few friends, happened to visit the Vic pub in Auckland, where she saw twenty-two-year-old Barry for the very first time. He was reciting the eye-watering poem 'The Ballad of Eskimo Nell'. It was a long and bawdy tale that Barry had become very proficient at telling. All who listened were amazed how well he remembered every word, and how well he told it; they loved it. Even though it was full of foul language, it never seemed to offend anybody. Mum was intrigued.

Barry was fresh out of the bush, where for several years he

had been in very remote areas of the New Zealand wilderness, hunting wild pigs and deer for the government. His meeting with Mum that Saturday night was to change his direction in life forever. Mum's friends soon became Barry's. He drank in the whole bohemian scene, along with a whole lot of whisky. He found it exciting.

It seemed the right thing to do, so Mum and Barry got married - both at just twenty-three years of age. The pair of them looked a little stunned on their wedding day at Astley Avenue.

Barry worked at a number of jobs and schemes - labouring, tree felling, driving trucks and trapping possums, to name just a few.

Mum became pregnant with Ivan. Barry wasn't so sure about city life; he wasn't so sure about married life either. They tried going bush together, where Barry was at his best.

Barry was so natural and at ease there - he could turn a piece of corrugated iron into a fireplace, a peach tin into a candle holder. A billy boiling over an open fire, and a yarn from the great storyteller himself. Mum often said you could heat your hands on Barry's warmth. He was like the salt in the stew - you need it.

When he drew you in with his charm and storytelling, when he had you at your most vulnerable, this is when he could be his most cruel, which Mum ultimately found out.

They barely hung in there together, Mum and Barry, between the break-ups and the make-ups. They fought a lot, and they could get physical. Mum wasn't shy about bashing Barry back either. She was tough.

In one particular fight, Barry threw a doughnut at Mum. It missed her and hit the wallpaper. The greasy shape of the doughnut would stay on the wall for the next twenty years, as

Astley Avenue.

the stain kept coming through each new layer of wallpaper that went up. We thought it was funny growing up and would tell our friends about it.

On another occasion they had decided to get back together, Barry came home for the big make-up and Mum had baked him a beautiful cake with 'I LOATHE YOU' iced on the top. He was furious. Apparently Mum wasn't quite over his cheating.

And she was now pregnant with me.

Barry was rarely at home, and a short few weeks before I was born, he left and would never return to the marriage. Apparently, Barry turned up at Saint Helens Hospital when I arrived but Mum told him to get back on his horse and piss off.

They did try one more time to make it work - or Mum did. They decided to meet at a friend's place in the Waitākeres. Mum had Ivan and I all dressed up, looking cute in the back seat of the car with a load of groceries that she had just bought. Surely he couldn't say no to this.

He didn't even turn up.

He'd been and gone and left a coat with £5 attached and a note: 'Sell the coat. I can't do this.'

They would both go on to marry others and have more children, but throughout their lives neither of them ever managed to completely let go of each other.

IVAN I was born in April 1958. According to Mum, I was a disturbed baby. Out of her five boys, I was the hardest to bring up. I was a disturbed child, as the psychiatrist once stated at school. Then I was a disturbed adolescent, and afterwards I became a disturbed adult.

I can't blame anyone else for that. Just my good luck.

It's manifested in many ways. I once looked up the qualities

Tina – Ivan and Martin's mum,
and Barry's first wife.

of a sociopath and was surprised at the similarities to my personality. I don't think there's anything external that caused it, though exasperation may have pushed me a bit that way.

I spent a fair bit of my life doing destructive things. I enjoyed being a vandal. It gave me great glee to fuck things up, and I had no discipline or guidance. I was allowed to behave badly, so I did.

There are many possible ways to describe my terrible behaviour. But the end result is that I was a massive cunt to the ones who relied on me.

It's not that I didn't *want* to be normal - I just couldn't do it. My brother Marty has been the opposite - a good dad, provider, and the rest. He's looked after me, alongside our truly awesome mother. Without her, I wouldn't have made it.

For a few years, more than once, I considered suicide.

ERIK I was born in 1965. Six weeks later, Mum took me to Holland to live with my grandmother, where we stayed for the next several years. I grew up speaking Dutch and enjoying treats like *drop* and *speculaas*. It wasn't until I was almost five that we returned to New Zealand, taking the long way by boat.

In Holland, Mum had told everyone that her husband was working back in New Zealand and was hoping to join us soon, but that was only so she wouldn't be shunned as a fallen woman in a land that was still very conservative.

In reality, they'd never been married. I was conceived in the back of a Volkswagen one night after a party, and Barry scarpered soon after he discovered Mum was pregnant.

Mum's a photographer, and I would often come along as she travelled the country in her Beetle, exploring and taking pictures. On one of these trips, she took me to meet Barry. Years later, she gave me a photo of the two of us, a small boy standing proudly beside a tall, smiling man, but I can't remember that day. It was the only time I ever met him.

In those early years, it was just me and Mum, and I was free to roam and play as I wanted. I revelled in the freedom.

'I was conceived in the back of a Volkswagen one night after a party, and Barry scarpered soon after he discovered Mum was pregnant.'

A few years later, she met another man and I gained a stepfather. At first, I gravitated towards this new man, who filled a Barry-shaped hole in my life. At one point, I even asked to take on his surname. But then my sister came along, and then my younger brother, and things changed. I found myself on the cutting edge of his vicious moods.

He would take off his belt and whack me for being too noisy, while his own children, playing alongside, were little angels who could do no wrong.

One Christmas, I was excited when he gave me a huge parcel. I tore off layer after layer of wrapping paper, only to find a scrubbing brush.

'You can use it to clean my car,' he said with a smirk.

Some years later, he threw all my clothes out of the second-storey window onto the driveway because he was sick of having me around.

He wore me down. A rough shell began to form around my heart to keep the pain at bay. Alone in my room, I would seethe with anger and despair, and even fantasised about killing him, so that I could be free.

Then finally, when I was in my early teens, we shifted to another house - just me, Mum, my sister and my brother.

At last. I could breathe again and slowly, gradually, I began to heal.

MARTIN We didn't have a lot growing up at Astley Avenue, but we were happy.

Mum's parties were something not to be missed. When I was just five years old, I should've been in bed, but I wasn't going to miss out on any of the fun. Besides, there was always a bowl of those little red polony sausages with tomato sauce, and I was having me some.

I can still clearly remember a particular night when our house was heaving with people, music, smoke, talking and laughter. I was in my pyjamas about to sneak another sausage when I was handed one with just the right amount of tomato sauce on it by a very kind man. I instantly liked him, and not just because he was giving me what I wanted. There was something about him. I trusted him.

He got me several sausages that night. Later that evening, I was sitting as happy as you like on his knee. It felt right, it *was* right.

Some weeks later the man was at our house again. After he

A young Lyall.

left, Mum announced to us all that she was going to marry him. And she did! Walter Lester - Wally - became my stepfather. Certainly a day to celebrate.

We all struck the jackpot to have such a decent, kind and wonderful man come and live with us. Mum chose well this time. And he wasn't just taking on Mum, but also Mum's two children born to the monster, and two more children to the famous Barry Crump.

The monster at this time was still coming to our house, bullying and menacing Mum.

On one occasion, the monster brought his brother. Wally took them both on, and it gave him a fight to remember. They smashed a heavy, jagged glass bowl on Wally's head, fracturing his skull. He was sitting in our wash house out the back with his hands on his head, blood dripping from in between his fingers. I asked Wally if he was all right. Without looking up, he told me it was just red ink and I was not to worry.

He was protecting me. He was protecting us. Although I was very young, I can still remember the gravity of the situation.

I was standing in the driveway with Mum when the police arrived to take the monster and his brother away.

The monster never returned to Astley Avenue.

I must thank Wally for the wonderful life he gave us; he worked so hard and provided for us all - took Mum on trips overseas, taught me how to cook, made us feel safe.

Wally and Mum would have two sons of their own: my younger brothers Guy and Morgan.

LYALL Mum was pregnant when she met Barry at the pub in Auckland on that sunny afternoon.

'What's your problem?' he asked, taking in her beauty

before staring at her swollen belly.

Love might not have been instant but the spark was born and by the next day they couldn't rid each other from their thoughts.

I don't remember Barry smashing Mum in the face and putting her in hospital. I didn't know about the violence he'd been through, nor did I know about Mum's pain of losing her mum and living in hardship and poverty.

This was in Waihī, where I lived with my brother Al, my mother and Barry, where the sun beamed on fresh grass and golden sands.

I hardly remember us sailing to Europe, going through the Suez Canal. There are only vague memories of the dope fields of Morocco.

I'm told Barry thought it funny to make me smoke hash. I was two years old and, understandably enough, Mum was horrified.

We once had dope drying on the bonnet of the Land Rover and the police pulled up behind us. Barry slammed on the brakes, sending the dope flying forward before coasting the car over the top of it and casually rolling open the window.

'Yeah, g'day mate . . .'

There are just-as-vague memories of me drinking beer, wearing lederhosen, drunkenly singing, at a pub in Germany in 1972. Then crying, being comforted by Dad, Mum and my brother, being smothered in love.

And then travelling again, through narrow country roads, alongside open fields, people shouting and crying, and, all of sudden, no Dad.

MARTIN I know now that Barry visited us on occasions, but I don't remember meeting my father until I was nine.

Lyall, in the striped shirt, with his brother Alan, Brenner Pass, Switzerland, 1972.

Mum had always tried to protect us from Barry, from his charm, from the promises he'd never keep, and from the hurt that would inevitably come.

It was May 1968. Barry was on the phone with Mum, and he asked her what I was up to. She told him I was interested in carpentry and doing well.

'Put Martin on the phone,' he said.

Mum handed me the phone and said, 'It's your father.'

'Mum had always tried to protect us from Barry, from his charm, from the promises he'd never keep, and from the hurt that would inevitably come.'

I instantly felt nervous.

'G'day mate. Our birthdays are pretty close together – I reckon we should go out and celebrate. What do you think?' Barry's birthday was on 15 May; mine is the 29th.

I went from nervous to impossibly excited. I said that I'd like that very much.

'I'll pick you up at six o'clock. We're going out for dinner and whatever else we feel like.'

I was excited for the rest of the day.

Six o'clock came and went, excitement now gone.

I was sound asleep when he turned up at 11pm. I woke up as he sat on the edge of my bed. He handed me two cold cheeseburgers and a hammer, then disappeared into the night.

I was sitting in the lounge at Astley Avenue when I next saw Barry, a few months later. He came in the front door and Ivan, who was just ten years old, started following Barry like a puppy - from the front door, past the lounge and kitchen. Ivan was bouncing around him, wanting his father's attention. They didn't see me watching.

Barry was in no mood for this as he made his way down the hallway, out to the backyard to where Mum was hanging clothes on the line. From the end of the hallway, I heard *whack!* Then I saw Ivan walking back into the kitchen with a look of such utter rejection and hurt.

Barry may as well have bashed me as well. I felt my brother's pain and I hated my father for it.

This is when I started to see what Mum had been protecting us from.

LYALL I carry memories from Hurst Green, Sussex and London, the seaside, kind people - Mum and Al, no Dad. I helped Mum pick strawberries; we were listening to the Beatles sing 'Lucy in the Sky with Diamonds', and I felt Mum's struggle and the bottomless love she had to give.

I must have been three when Mum took me up the lane and across the busy road to the kindergarten. I learned to talk and be with the other kids. Al only went there for a little while. I think he ended up going to the bigger kids' school, where he made friends with the mean boys. I guess that was when I realised we were somehow different to each other.

Barry, Vanda, Alan (left) and Lyall,
Piccadilly Circus, London, 1972.

Mum made friends with a man who gave us presents.

I painted myself with the hash oil he'd left out when he and Mum went for a walk. When they got back, he was so angry he thrashed me with his belt. I cried and missed Dad as Mum cleaned me up. Al had told me not to play with that stuff.

All of a sudden, we were back in Morocco - the police again. Not fun this time: jail for having seven kilos of high-grade hashish lashed under the car.

I had my fourth birthday in that jail. The moustached guard gave me a matchbox.

The guy Mum had met took the rap - we were out, and Barry came to get us. I was so happy to see him, smell him and hold him. We were going home, but I didn't remember where that was.

The first sign I was disturbed was when I made a house from envelopes under my bed, then lit it on fire. I didn't utter a word of warning to anyone - just carried on as normal, playing with my brother in the lounge.

If my new dad hadn't moved so quickly, it would have burned the house down and possibly even killed us all.

I didn't know or care about his history. All I knew was that he was my new dad, a different shape from the last one but somehow the same, even better.

It was 1975 and we were back in New Zealand when I first met him, at the age of five: a solid bloke, a builder, surfer, world traveller - and my new dad. I loved him straight away.

He took us on adventures, camping at his favourite surf spots, tenting around a fire, swimming in the ocean, riding the waves on our foam boards, making new friends at every small town. It was a different life to the one I'd imagined with Barry.

My new dad showed surf films and made ads for television. I got the idea that I might be an advertising guy, write the ads

Barry does the washing,
Morocco, 1972.

or something - make him proud of me.

Our new dad took Al and me to Huntly and we carefully dismantled an old farmhouse. Al and I loved it, getting grubby and bonding with our new dad.

He took me to Hamilton on my own once, to see a surf movie called *The Endless Summer*.

I was lost between two worlds: one steady with Mum, my new dad and Al; the other with Barry and his mysterious world of writing and hunting, being at the pub, smoking rollies, drinking beer and whisky, telling tall yarns, being a central and iconic character.

I think we enjoyed living in Herne Bay in Auckland, me and my new family. We made friends and explored and I got in the habit of finding things - money, jewellery. I'd pick up anything that looked useful or interesting. We were losing our British accents and settling in to being Kiwi.

We could feel the loving anticipation, the winds of change. This time, though, we were wary, experienced, tainted.

I could say that it was Barry's father's fault for being so tough on him. And his father could say that he was who he was because *his* father was affected by his involvement in the war.

Now I was lighting a house of envelopes under my bed and I didn't know why.

'Could you make us a sandwich?' Al asked our new dad when we first met him. He smiled kindly. He was great.

'Sure, what do you want on it?'

'Jam,' I said eagerly. Then I hugged him. He pulled away. His smile faded and he hurried off to make our sandwiches.

I told him about the time a rat had taken a jam sandwich from my hand when we were living in England. Al told him about the bird-eating spider we saw living in the high corner of a toilet block in Morocco.

He took us on an adventure through the bush on a long, winding, narrow and dusty road out to the west coast - Piha. This was the place, he said. It's where the dream began. A new beginning where they could let their love grow and flow.

He was amazing, my new dad.

He built us a cool house. His friends were nice and they made friends with Mum.

She started a business in the rag trade downstairs. Our rooms were next to it, by the old wringer washing machine.

Mum learned to surf and taught us. We lived halfway up the hill, just down from Pendrell Road, below the top rock - an old magma chamber from one of the many extinct volcanos that circle and look down at the beaches and relentless waves of the Pacific Ocean.

The bus ride to Oratia School was a long, loud, bumpy journey. Al remembered that Barry's brother lived close to the school.

'What are you buggers doing here? Why don't you stuff off - you don't belong around here!'

'Come on, Lyall. He doesn't love us.'

We knew in our hearts that Barry and his family were not ours. Our family was out at Piha.

I was eleven and into drumming. Dad bought me a small kit. I ended up having to move it to the neighbour's place - a full-blown alcoholic, complete with crazy mates and a piano. The man was a musical genius and taught me all sorts of beats. He taught me a lot of things actually, and so did his wild and drunken friends. I learnt a bit about the blues, classical and operatic music.

He also taught me a bit about crazy - how to go there but also how to come back. It was a scary sort of place: windows closed, curtains drawn, citrus rotting, bread baking, clutter and full ashtrays. He would often send me on the dreaded long walk down to the shop to buy him and his pal cigs.

IVAN Barry was an awesome dad to many children, just not his own. Apart from the fact that he always shot through, no matter who from, his own kids were just too much for him.

Having said that, he did once come to the family home to get me and take me with him. My mother seriously threatened to put an axe in his head. He got the message loud and clear.

A day at the beach – Barry, Lyall (right) and his brother Alan.

3.

Choose Your Own Adventure

Living with Barry's absence

'I didn't like myself, and I missed Barry.'

ERIK Back then, Mum was a free spirit, a part of the Wellington art scene, and she would sometimes hold parties at our house.

Once, when I was about twelve, a guest came into my bedroom and sat on the bed beside me. I didn't understand what was going on at the time, but I didn't like this man sitting too close, his fingers tracing patterns on my bare thighs as they nonchalantly crept towards my pyjama shorts.

Mum came in, said that he was naughty, and told him to go back to the party. But I knew what abuse felt like. It wasn't the only time.

In later years, I began to wonder how different my life might have been if I'd had a father to protect me from things like this.

MARTIN Ivan and I both got in trouble now and again – at times the police were involved, mostly for minor infringements. Then I got caught for car conversion.

A couple of mates and I pinched a car off a car dealer who we knew didn't behave too well. A bit like us, really. We had that little red Ford Anglia for a few days, joyriding around the district in it, then left it on the side of the road.

Someone dobbed us in. I was arrested and chucked in a cell at the central police station, so Mum came and picked me up.

She drove home with her right hand on the wheel. Her left hand was free, and unfortunately she was left-handed - she bashed me all the way home.

Then she did something way worse than walloping me. She sat me down at the kitchen table and cut all my hair off. I had long hair at the time, which was very important to me. I was so upset. As I lay smouldering in my room, Mum came in and said, 'I love you, by the way.'

'In later years, I began to wonder how different my life might have been if I'd had a father to protect me from things like this.'

Later that night, I jumped out of my bedroom window and it was five days later when Mum finally found me on the streets of New Lynn.

Even then, I knew she had only done it out of love and fear I would go down the wrong path.

Wally never hit us and never needed to, because Mum dished out the punishment for us all - and she could be very scary. She had a row of big leather belts with studs and buckles on her bedroom wall. While these were a part of her wardrobe, she would also use them to keep her large boys in line, but by then we had outgrown this punishment. It was having no effect.

One day, Mum was thrashing a belt around my legs when she looked up at me, and I was just looking down at her, waiting for her to finish.

'I don't think we will do this anymore,' she said, huffing and puffing.

The belts were only for decoration after that.

Ivan and I are both over six feet tall and would go on to have some hairy moments, including clashes with local gangs who saw us as easy targets - just part of growing up in West Auckland at the time. It was only after we stood up for ourselves that we began to be left alone.

In fine family tradition, Ivan was kicked out of school at fourteen, which is sad because he has a brain like no other. If they had handled him right, he could have been some academic type, but it was not to be.

We didn't have to wait long before I followed the family tradition as well - I wasn't so much kicked out as politely asked to leave, also at just fourteen. I got a legal exemption from school but had to tell my true age if I was to find a job.

So, I was off to farm in the small community of Piopio, in the King Country, where I would do a whole lot more growing up. I didn't last long. I learned a lot but milking the house cow by hand at five every morning was quite a shock to a city boy like me. More than that, I knew it wasn't my future.

I headed back to Auckland. I was still only fourteen and needed a job, so now I needed to lie about my age. No trouble to me. I'm sorry to admit it, but I'm very good at lying.

I landed myself a job in Newmarket, at Joseph Lucas Industries, a company that dealt in spare parts for cars. I'd been there no more than a couple of weeks when I walked into the area where the public could order and purchase car parts. I saw a man who looked very familiar to me, just standing there.

It looked like Barry - he had a handlebar moustache, but what put me off was that the man was gaunt, thin-looking. I waited for him to get to the counter so I could hear him speak - I would know for sure when he talked. It was him.

At this point, he was aware of me staring at him, something no doubt he was used to. He turned to me, not recognising me - well, why should he? The last time he saw me, I was a child. Standing in front of him now, I was six feet two and fifteen stone, but still just fourteen years old.

'Can I help you?' he asked.

'Your name Barry?'

'Yeah.'

'I'm your son, Martin,' I said, and put my hand out for him to shake.

He was definitely taken aback by this. He stuttered and stammered, not sure what to do with me.

He took my phone number, promised this and that, but nothing came of it. He couldn't do it.

The truth was that he didn't need to do anything with me. But it was all too much for him - he was gone. It would be another four years before we met again.

The family had a catering business at this time, and it came to include a couple of shops in the city. During the mid- to late 1970s, on Saturday mornings, Ivan and I had the honour of running our takeaway shop.

We had noticed these two little fellas coming in with big beaming smiles on their faces, ordering their food and chatting away to us. I began to ask a question or two of them and, over the course of a week or so, I found out their mum's name was Vanda.

I now knew who these wonderful little guys were - they were our brothers, Barry's son Lyall and his brother to a different dad, Alan.

After this revelation, their food became free of charge, which made us even more popular with our new brothers Alan and Lyall. Vanda was running a stall at the markets, not far away from us, so we saw them most weekends.

Just as it happened to Ivan and me, a very good man would come into Alan and Lyall's lives - a stepfather of the best kind.

I have no doubt that they have their scars, but as long as we have good men in our lives to lean on, we needn't become victims of our upbringing.

LYALL Mum and Dad had a stall at Cook Street Market, in the centre of town by Aotea Square, selling clothes and quilts that they had made. Our stall was next to the big Buddha at a place called The Centre of the World, and across from a clothing stall run by a strange man. There was a constant blend of human voices, footsteps, incense and food smells. A world far away from a father I'd almost forgotten.

Al was becoming super smart; I was highly emotional. We seemed to be fighting a lot but still enjoyed adventures around Queen Street, the wharf, Albert Park, the museum and, most of all, to the movies. Every weekend was the same - into town, movies, selling at the market, puff on bidi herbal cigarettes, then wait for Mum and Dad to finish having drinks at the pub, before we'd make the long drive back to Piha.

'You know your brothers have a food caravan on Durham Street, don't you?' Mum asked one Saturday morning at the market.

'We have . . . brothers?' Al asked.

'Martin and Ivan, yes. They make burgers and chips and stuff. Here, have an extra five dollars. Go and get lunch there.'

I overheard the conversation but was looking at the Buddha, wondering why he smiled, wondering what my brothers might look like and sound like.

They gave us a free feed and seemed nice. Martin told me Al wasn't Barry's son; that he and Ivan were my true brothers. I was confused and felt more lost than ever. I argued and fought with Al with extra meaning from then on. It was his fault we weren't with Barry.

Gratitude with grace
The middle of the race
The chosen few
The ones that knew
The power of love
That perfect glove

As a kid I went to Oratia School and really liked it there - a lot of history, neat teachers and I got to hang out with my cousin Warren, who I'd seen on the occasional visit with Mum when we went to see Barry. Warren sometimes got us the strap but was fun and big and loving.

I drew mazes on the raw Gib downstairs at home. I was drawn into the bush under the top rock, where I built huts. I made origami sculptures and threw paper darts off the rock. Sometimes, they'd glide into the Glen Esk Valley, flying free over the tops of kauri trees in the Waitākere bush. Other times, they'd drift down toward home and the road. I could feel things up there, maybe smell them - hear the echoes from the past, from people I didn't know.

Somehow, I talked with the bush and the land with my

thoughts, and I could hear it whispering back.

I brought people to my special places, like the hollow kauri tree on the other side of the ridge. The kōwhai grove and mini top rock, with a view into the valley. The cave under the cliff and the massive pūruri tree that jutted out of the slope into the tops of ponga and supplejack. The old skidder track gouged into the hill where they dragged up the majestic kauri trunks harvested by people from yesteryear.

'Somehow, I talked with the bush and the land with my thoughts, and I could hear it whispering back.'

Mum's brother and his friends built a way up to the first branch of the hollow kauri. I think they built a swing off of the pūruri tree, too. That pūruri tree was magnificent. Sitting among the lichen thirty metres off the ground was another world. Spiders and centipedes, kererū, fantails, kāhu.

The 'top rock' was part of a bigger mass of rock that dominated the ridge. Unpassable gorse and vague traces of an old tramline going up the flat ridge. Butterflies and rainbows, possums and dope patches covered in chicken wire.

This was the peaceful world I found, giving me a space between the worlds of my arguing parents.

Our new dad got a Bedford van and we seemed to be constantly on the move. I became good at swimming and body surfing; Al got a proper surfboard and started surfing out the back with the adults.

We surfed all the great spots around the North Island, from Ahipara and Shipwreck Bay to Māhia Peninsula and Tolaga Bay, and back up the East Coast to Whitianga and Whangamatā - making friends, showing movies.

I was eight years old when we did our first winter away in the mountains of the South Island. We skied at every club field on the island before moving on and spending the remaining months of winter in the campground at the bottom of the mountain road leading up to Tūroa on Mount Ruapehu.

The next winter we had a new brother - the apple of Dad's eye and a great reason to stop the constant arguing with Al. Maybe I wasn't so lost between these two worlds - this was it, my family.

Things seemed different at Piha. Al had his surfer mates and his girlfriends. I made friends with a local family. They seemed perfect - they had a swimming pool, they took me to judo on Thursdays after school, they took me to surf carnivals where their two boys and I competed as Nippers.

For some reason, I began distancing myself from my real family. There was even talk of adoption. I was so lost and constantly sought places and means to escape, like the top rock, my mazes, my model aircraft, the neighbours' big old bike.

Dad seemed keen to work me. Moving sticks of wood, cleaning bricks, scraping paint - he once had me stay home from school to excavate a used long-drop toilet. It taught me resilience but it grew a burning resentment towards my new dad, and I was often an emotional mess. It came to a head when he arrived outside the other family's house, screaming and yelling.

Apparently, the mother had stolen money, which really sent them to the cleaners. We all hid quietly in the dark but Dad broke into the house and ranted angrily like a bad-smelling bomb. He soon left.

One day I was on my way home from school on the bus, just another ordinary day, when, to my surprise, I saw Mum and Dad at the Anawhata turn-off. The Beddy looked full. Mum came onto the bus and gave me a letter and a hug and said a heartfelt goodbye.

Al knew what was going on, but I didn't. We were on our own. Mum and Dad had gone skiing for the winter. The guy they called Ears was to look after us - a vegetarian hippie with plenty of rice and lentils to give.

One night, when he had got us stoned, I noticed he had ears that stuck out from his head. I had to go down into my room because I couldn't stop laughing.

My dyslexia kicked in around the time my parents left, but I guess it had always been an issue for me. Life was a flow of booze and drug-filled parties; surf, sun and rain; wind, sandflies and streams; the bush, hippies and surfers; uncles, the market and money.

Our parents came back from the winter's skiing; they left us again the next winter - this time with Mum's brothers and their friends. That simply meant more days off school enjoying the land and ocean, the bush and birdlife.

I had developed a mean streak that I pushed onto my younger brother. I almost killed him a few times. I could blame Barry for my meanness. He surely had something to do with it.

Luckily, my young brother is okay - the worst he came away with was a scar on his lip. I didn't love him as much as I should have. I was twelve and felt like I was having a divorce from my family.

Al's surfer mate from America had some acid called Purple Haze. Al convinced him to give me a bit. Wow, the stars were bright that night. They spoke to me like the bush and ocean did. My body vibrated like the snare of my drum and I loved myself feeling so good. I just wanted to run and be free.

'All they saw in me was an utter bastard. In some small way, I had achieved my destiny of becoming just like my father, the great Barry Crump.'

I started to surf more seriously. I'll never forget my first wave. I'd ridden waves before, body surfing, but this was different. I stood up this time. The feeling is indescribable - the flow, the smell, the sound. I was hooked. I fell in love and was fascinated; it was as though the wave embraced me and loved me back.

It was the same feeling as Barry or Mum or Dad or my brothers loving me. It all made sense. The ocean swallowed the pain. I'd found my calling and made a pledge to dedicate my life to the ocean. It and the land were my new parents, ready to shape and mould me.

Dad got me a ten-speed bike. A Raleigh. My new obsession. I rode that thing up the valley to North Piha and up the hill, down and back up again. The hill was no longer an issue, and I had a new dream and a reason to push myself hard.

I planned to ride to school and back. My new friend came with me. He stole a cheque from a milk bottle on the way up the hill and we tried to cash it when we got into Oratia. The police pulled us over when we were riding home up Forest Hill Road.

The cop was trying to be heavy. I was in big trouble and got given a letter from school to give to my parents. I threw it out the bus window but somehow it was found and given to Mum. I thought it was no big deal and that everything was basically okay. It wasn't. That was the beginning of the violent, aggressive and destructive path that I'd always seemed determined to go down.

My disturbing behaviour progressed, and manifested into bullying and beating my fellow students. I learnt how to use my words and body to hurt people the way I had been hurt and rejected, in the vain hope they could understand what hurt me.

No one did. All they saw in me was an utter bastard. In some small way, I had achieved my destiny of becoming just like my father, the great Barry Crump.

The tail of love is conflict
Confusing, crushing, causing chaos
A failing flee from what seems real

I could feel the heat of hate's arrows piercing me as I grew older. Various forms of violence came with it - a turmoil of lies and conflict, stealing and copying other people's lives.

I didn't like myself, and I missed Barry.

I was so lost and lovesick; my behaviour was becoming out of control. I had peaks of crazy that involved glass, blood and pain.

The school social was the sacred and special event of the year. I was the thirteen-year-old punk who orchestrated its demise. I created anarchy – turned off the lights and started a food fight, ruining the night. I was ejected with happy madness, applause and shocked sadness. I sure showed them toffs.

Something had to break. I was a lying, stealing cheat and I needed a stern voice. I needed someone to follow and look up to.

Dad couldn't stand my lying and stealing, and he couldn't work me hard enough. Mum was at a breaking point because of my behaviour and Al was busy with his girlfriend and mates and being grown up. I was still a child needing a hug.

One day, the police turned up at school. A wrinkly old guy and a sharp lady. The two school deans were there, too. I don't know how long the interrogation lasted but I broke. They broke me. My little gang followed as I left. I saw them briefly on the way out, went home, and didn't say a thing to my parents.

Two weeks later, Dad got a phone call from someone at the Henderson police station.

'Yes . . . yes . . . yes, he's right here. No . . . no . . . he didn't tell us that. Okay. I'll have a word to him . . . okay, thanks. Okay, okay. Yes . . . okay, bye. Thanks again.' Clang.

'You little rat!' Dad said, before giving me a hiding. Al pushed me down the stairs and gave me a kick. Mum cried.

In a hateful fury, I ran up to the top rock and waited till the sun was about to sink past the ocean.

Later on, I snuck back and into my room. No dinner that

night. I missed Barry and thought about what life would have been like if I had lived with him.

The next day, Dad took me over to a gorse patch on Lone Kauri Road. He left me with a saw, an axe and a grubber. I cut gorse until the spiders scared me out of there. I stashed the tools and walked the long, winding gravel road back up to Piha Road.

As I walked toward Piha itself, I looked out over the bush, and it dawned on me. An idea, something I could do that would solve everything. I began to ponder the different ways I could do it, but the bush was telling me not to. The mere thought somehow freed my mind. Even if I wasn't actually going to follow through, I now realised that I could give up any worry that I had done anything terrible - nothing seemed to matter, and I was free.

It was a long walk to Pendrell Road from Lone Kauri. I heard Dad on the phone to Barry - he wouldn't have me. Then I heard him call a friend of the family. I was to go and live with a lady and her son in Sandringham.

I was there for about a month before she flipped out at me for stealing and lying - again - and packed me up and threw me on a bus back to Piha.

No one really talked to me.

'How will I ever make this better, Mum?'

'Time is a great healer, Lyall. It'll be okay.'

I wanted to know when. How long would I have to wait? Mum was as nice as she could be. I settled on the idea it didn't matter anyway, seeing as I was going to die.

Later on, I had to wait outside while Mum and Dad attended a hearing at the school. In solemn, sulky silence, we drove home.

'You've been expelled. We'll enrol you at Green Bay. There is a teacher who drives from out our way but you'll have to meet him at the start of Lone Kauri. You can either hitch up or catch the bus. Up to you,' Dad said.

'Whatever . . . I'll hitch.'

So, I hitched, and first up got a ride with Dad's mate, who gently told me off the whole way to Lone Kauri. I think he could tell I didn't care about what he said.

The teacher seemed stressed. He clearly didn't like the idea of me catching a ride with him. He pretended he had barely enough gas to get him to the school; kept telling me they don't pay much. I assured him I would get him gas money but decided I'd try and hitch all the way next time.

I would imagine Barry driving up and stopping. Me getting in and rolling smokes for us. It was often a long time between rides and if it rained I got wet . . . making it harder again to get a ride. If the surf was good, I'd just head down to the beach and surf all day.

That summer, I went on my first surf trip down to Gisborne. When I got home, Dad told me not to bother unpacking, that I could go and stay with my mates. They lived in Glen Esk Valley and accepted me immediately. I'd left school and they helped me get on the dole and took me surfing.

I still kept an eye out for Barry's red truck in the vain hope he might magically appear, roll me a smoke and take me to the pub for a smoked fish and mussel pie.

Al once came on a surf trip with me, to Shipwreck Bay. It was great surf but he also let me have it, told me his truth and that I'd let him down.

He got himself so angry and drunk on that long drive back to Auckland that he turned to punch me, but accidentally punched his girlfriend in the face. I refused to go anywhere with him again after that.

I have known great love and generosity from my brother Martin. At this stage I hadn't seen him since him I was at Green Bay High School. It was dole day. I had my big coat on and was carrying my food in bags, walking across the New Lynn bus station on my way back to Piha. I was contemplating the hitch when a booming voice hit my ears. Martin.

He took me in, fed me - food and love - and gave me a motorbike and a pair of Red Band gumboots. It was the happiest I'd been in ages, in the heart of a cold, wet and miserable winter.

I was eventually pulled over by the police and, not having a licence, had to give the bike back, but it had opened a door into Martin's heart and was the start of a friendship that I sorely needed.

I turned seventeen and celebrated by going for a surf at a beach called Whites, where I'd almost been eaten by a shark.

I had become a surf fiend - that's all I wanted to do, it's all I knew. So when my dad turned up at the beach and asked for my help one day, I wasn't keen but I did it, and soon realised why he'd been gathering building materials for all those years. He had another dream. This time, in a small village called National Park.

I helped him build a house with Mum's brother, and found that he and Mum had forgiven me. The truth was that they were alarmed at my having given up on society, on life.

Dad pestered me to do some course and become a builder or something. My resentment, my rage, began to swell again. I couldn't take it. I became self-destructive and took it out on the ocean. My approach to big-wave surfing was manic. I had a private battle; I was at war. Me against the world - and I was losing and getting hurt. I didn't know if I could face another winter at Piha.

Mum and Dad had been around the world with my younger

brother. Time and distance had softened things and Mum felt love for me again.

She organised a course for me down the hill from National Park, in a place called Raurimu. It was called an access course, and was with an outfit called Plateau Guides. They taught us to rock climb, ride horses, kayak and raft rivers, trek over mountains and explore caves. They taught me to explore myself.

I soon found myself fighting for my life again - literally. This time on the upper reaches of the Motu River. I had become stuck under my raft in a rapid in the tight crevice of a rock.

We were taking turns at being the leader of the boat and shouting the right commands to see us through the grade-four rapids safely. I negotiated this kind of double-slot rapid with the team, my new family, and we decided on the right channel that fed away from the cliff. We became wedged.

Jim, the older guy, and another began working the side pontoon up. We were shouting, trying to stay calm, but an air of panic crept over us like a hail. I was the leader. I was strong but not savvy and decided the boat needed a nudge from behind . . . my feet were instantly swept under the jammed boat.

If it were just the boat, I could have easily slithered under and out the other end, but this boat was laden, the water angry and filling the raft. I held on against the flow of water as my brain fought for a solution. No one realised I was gone. My family - I needed to alert them. I needed my family.

Air was millimetres away from my mouth. With the last of my strength, I pulled my head above the unrelenting water and screamed, then let myself relax.

As a surfer, I knew I had one good gulp of air and I couldn't waste it by struggling. The team now knew I was in peril. As I hung onto that rope, I could hear Jim take command; they let down a thwart and worked as a team on the right side of the boat. I could see the article in the paper about this keen surfer who died on the river, but I really wanted to live.

I let go of the rope and once again gave in. I stopped fighting and let the great river take me away. At the same time, the team jerked the side of the boat up and I washed through underneath. I swam that long rapid and drifted to a spot the team could pick me up from. The moment somehow shaped me, teaching me something, as though the river had spoken its wisdom to me.

'I let go of the rope and once again gave in. I stopped fighting and let the great river take me away.'

On the long drive back to Raurimu, we stopped in at Barry's mate's place and found Barry himself. He was loud and charismatic in front of my course mates and teachers. I felt somehow embarrassed to be proud of him and left his mate's house half drunk, and confused by questions I couldn't answer. I selfishly wished I'd died on the Motu.

But mostly, they were golden times that gave me hope. I applied for a job doing rentals at the Whakapapa ski field, where Dad had taught us to ski. Al worked there, too, in the ski workshop, and Dad worked as a cleaner. Slowly we became a family again.

Lyall takes flight on the slopes.

It was apparent though that I wasn't normal. People labelled me and I deserved it. I was 'out there', 'crazy', 'off the dial', a liability and a dangerous person. Like the ocean, the mountain was big enough to hide me. It spoke to me, shaping me, teaching me. Not before it tried to kill me, though.

And my river of hate still raged - at Al and Dad and Barry. I couldn't find love, only cold, hard, lonely pain. I still had healing to do.

Dad got me a job in Auckland in the demolition trade. I thought I was strong but it turned out I wasn't. It was a great place to start, though. I worked and hurt and struggled and climbed and almost got killed and no one cared - it was great.

I loved it and slowly began to love myself. I began to explore some of the nicer things about myself. I grew a shield for the taunts to bounce off, and I even attracted the attention of the media. Ginette McDonald tracked me down on a demolition site at Auckland Girls' Grammar. She was working on a Lynn of Tawa show called *In Search of the Great New Zealand Male*, and Ginette and her crew wanted to know what was in the heart of the great Barry Crump's son. Like him, I charmed them with lies and didn't really let anyone in.

Before long, I began to self-destruct again and needed pain. I leaned into the ocean. I asked of the bush and found myself in the mountains and rivers of the central North Island. I became employed with Plateau Guides as a raft guide. Al did the access course that year, too.

I worked on the mountain again, this time as a lift operator. I was moving up and moving inside myself, learning what it was like to be me. I found out that I was brave, reckless, verging on suicidal. I began jumping off the cliffs of Whakapapa. One jump I did was too big and I knocked myself out. A couple of ski patrollers saw me and were convinced I was trying to commit suicide.

I taught my younger brother how to jump cliffs and I realised that Barry had touched this young man through me - if it weren't for Barry being who he was, I wouldn't have been who I was, teaching my brother to be fearless.

The private parts of my body
Only I know where they go
Over ridges, into gullies
Across the Ruapehu snow.

I wasn't kind on myself but I did get better at skiing. People began to notice my skills and show me respect, something new for me. I gained friendships that grew each winter - people who actually liked and admired me. I drank that admiration like it was the elixir of life, as though it was the key to the answers I had been asking of myself all those years.

Eventually, being a lift operator started getting to me. I noticed the ski instructors had a good time on the mountain and lined myself up for a try-out. Four seasons on the lifts was enough.

I had made it into my early twenties and managed to gain entry into the exclusive world of the ski instructors - a scumbag loser from the depths of desperado ally into the uniform of the elite I didn't deserve. They knew it and some resented me, until I realised it myself as well.

Memories are chemical erosion, eroding moments
Turning them
Twisting them
binding them into the rope of life.

I was beginning to understand that love wasn't something I took; instead, it was something given, and it was reflected back by those who saw it.

I grew to love a girl and took her away from my stinking world of hate to Motueka, where we picked apples and enjoyed our time together, living with a guy named Bok and his dog Tuk, and a few other lost dope smokers.

This girl once got me to keep an eye out while she snuck away to go to the toilet in the orchard. Tuk came and ate it, then later Bok roared into the drive and leapt out of his Holden ute.

'What's the matter?' she asked.

'Tuk's puked and it smells like shit!'

We hid and laughed and loved some more. I kept writing to her even after we had split up. One day, her father replied telling me she had leukaemia. She died a year later.

I kept asking of the rivers and streams of Whakapapa. One day, on the start of the Whakapapaiti, below Matariki Falls, another guide and I sent a student and teacher down the first rapid. They fell out and vanished. One minute turned into ten, with no trace of them.

Panic gripped my heart and the tone of my voice. My head spun with the thought of killing these people.

After fifteen minutes that felt like an hour, they staggered back upstream. They had been sucked into a cave under the cliff and fought their way out fifty metres down. Flashes of the smiling Buddha in The Centre of the World at Cook Street Market kept flashing into my mind for the rest of the trip. *Why was he smiling?* I wondered.

'Put the piton eye through the carabiner attached to the harness. Make an Italian half-hitch to go over the piton . . . got it?'

'Yes,' I lied. The first few over the Whakapapa dam were fine.

The next few not, as the piton fell onto the rocks below. If the knot on the safety rope had failed, it could have killed the kid.

We got back to Raurimu and I announced that I was quitting the outdoors.

I had become dangerously overconfident and contented. My workmate at the ski school was amazed that I surfed in the summers and skied in the winters. I had seen the shape of myself but didn't notice the raging stream of anger eroding the earth I stood on. I was still financially insecure and being a ski instructor and dole-bludger didn't help.

I had done the line four times before: traverse toward McKenzie's Mistake, duck the safety rope, quick sharp turns on the steep shoulder line, up the chute into the frozen waterfall, jump the ledge and bask in the glory.

'Do it again, mate. I'll film you,' said a workmate.

I gave extra effort on the sharp turns. My ski tips crossed and I fell forward, straight for the edge of the cliff. In my mind, it was close to a thirty- or forty-metre drop onto a mogul field below. I tried slowing down, with my arms outstretched. They hit the rock edge, spiralling my body into space.

Was this it? I thought. *Is this the answer? My life in a wheelchair?*

I was reminded of when I did judo - third in Auckland, a formidable opponent and very good at break falls. Like the time I dropped from the ceiling and the girl pulled away the mats. I had to do a break fall, the best one I'd ever done.

Somehow time slowed, giving me time to get my balance. I saw the rock I would hit and executed the perfect break fall.

'Check his hip out!' shouted someone from the chairlift.

It must have looked and sounded as though I had cracked my hip into bits on that rock, but it was the sound of the tails of my skis hitting the rock, springing the bindings of my boots. If I hadn't done anything, yes, my hip would have been shattered. I'd realised that I had to move my legs and arch my back, bringing my arms into an arc, so I slapped the rock with my hands and heels with all my strength.

I was happy as soon as I came off the rock. I knew I was okay. Sore hands, but I was fine.

I ran up the slope to get my gear. People thought I was running on adrenaline and made me lie down. Mum and Dad took me into Taumarunui Hospital. The X-rays came back a negative and it was my shout for fish and chips.

'I had seen the shape of myself but didn't notice the raging stream of anger eroding the earth I stood on.'

I began winning ski races, giving me more confidence in myself - but something was missing. I ended up asking a wonderfully beautiful woman to marry me. It was Alan's girlfriend's sister, who they had set me up with.

She agreed, but it was only months later that we had an ugly, violent fight with Al and his missus over money. I knew that I still had issues to resolve - the raging river kept eroding the bank.

I took Mum for granted, I guess. She was such a solid rock that I thought she'd never crumble.

Mum is amazing, so amazing I could never adequately explain how and why. I cry even now as I dip my toe into the shallows of the depth of her love.

A portrait of Barry (found under the seat of a truck in the Far North a decade after his death).

4.

Growing Pains

Living with Barry's presence

'I must have been four years old and didn't know what a man was, let alone a father.'

LYALL It was pretty obvious that my parents would stay apart, but at least I got to see Barry. When I was eight or nine he let us stay with him at Oratia, in the bush next to a vineyard. Al got sick on the field mushrooms. I loved them.

Barry would play his guitar and sing about a fox, pausing to rap his knuckles on the wood of the guitar for effect, mesmerising us - well me, anyway. I think Al was just pissed at him for ditching us. I didn't care.

He tried explaining what God was, made us a cool rope swing, washed us in a forty-four-gallon drum, put us in the curl of a nīkau frond and slid us down a place we called Pine Needle Hill, and let us slide down the tray of the truck as it tipped its load and got too steep to hold on. He took us into the studio and we got on telly. He introduced us to cousins and uncles, gave us a friend in the form of a horse and its foal. He got angry with me for walking behind it. I didn't mind - it somehow made me love him even more.

HARRY I didn't grow up with my father. When I was introduced to him, by my mother, it didn't go well.

I must have been four years old and didn't know what a man was, let alone a father.

Then there was this huge, gesticulating person on our back doorstep, shouting words I didn't know the meaning of. In retrospect - a hard thing to quantify - I think the words might have been 'bloody' and 'bugger'.

I can still see the pink flowers and feel the cloth of my mother's dress, which I hid behind.

Mum was always keen for me to know my father. I was smitten by the idea of him.

Some time later, Mum shipped me off for a few days to a bush farm owned by a guy named Bill Arm, where Barry was staying in a hut. I must have been about ten.

I was as happy as a puppy. I loved the outsized hut - the fire, the smell of kerosene, the deep voice and the large hands of a man, the way I had to climb up to a loft on a makeshift ladder to sleep in smelly sheepskins.

Barry would tell me stories, such as the one about the ghost of the Māori chief who walked up to the hut at night, wailing. Or the woman in nightclothes who would appear at the bush line - pause for a moment - then turn and walk back into the bush. My father seemed to find her story more scary than any of the others he told. I wonder now whether it was just too close to home - 'going bush' - or echoed some sense of abandonment.

Another time, Barry left me alone and in charge of his dog Niff - some kind of bastardisation of the word 'communist'. He had gone for 'supplies' and took his rifle, and said he'd be back in a couple of hours.

Two days I waited with the mist and the fog twisting across the valley at night. I was never taught how to light a fire. My fear was not that a ghost would come out of the mist, but that it wouldn't.

Barry eventually came back with fresh strawberries, potatoes and a woman who looked like a hippie and smelled like herbs.

My father told me to close my eyes and open my mouth. Instead of a strawberry with cream, he put in my mouth a raw baby potato covered in shaving cream. It wasn't until my twenties that I reflected that this was not a funny joke and that he probably wanted me to go away. I was so 'dad struck' at the time, I thought it was funny and clever. Children and puppies must be pre-programmed with an extended benefit of the doubt.

'Mum was always keen for me to know my father. I was smitten by the idea of him.'

IVAN My first definitive memory of my father is from when I was about four years old. I remember feeling an unstoppable wave of needy emotion, running up to Barry, then getting a clout on the head and running away. The devastation at that age was huge; I can barely articulate it, but it had a profound effect on me. I might have been a very different person if he had simply ruffled my hair instead, and said something like, 'I'll just talk to your mother first.' Who can really say?

I felt the need for a father keenly and swore to myself that I would never abandon my own children. Something I did do.

Some of my children got to suffer my demented, damaging version of being a dad. The lucky ones escaped. In hindsight, the famous 20/20 vision of the past, if Barry had been around, he would have been terrible.

Barry wouldn't allow Martin and me to call him Dad, so we never did. It was just Barry. He was conspicuous by his absence.

One night, we were in our beds, and he came in and said, 'I'm fucked,' then went out again. A rare moment, but honest, that was to keep us going for a few years.

'I remember feeling an unstoppable wave of needy emotion, running up to Barry, then getting a clout on the head and running away.'

MARTIN The year was 1964 - Ivan was six years old, I was five. Our family had just purchased our first television set. We would often watch a programme called *Town and Around*, a current affairs show that aired right after the news. One particular night, Mum pointed to the TV: 'That's your father.'

There was Barry, standing next to a bride in front of a Land Rover with the bonnet up. He ripped a piece off her wedding dress and wiped the oil off the dipstick.

Barry would go on to do many comedy skits on the show. In one I remember watching, he had a female friend sit in a Land Rover while he hooked up a tow rope to tow her away. What she didn't know was that the vehicle had been cut into two, right behind the driver's seat, so when he drove off, more than half her vehicle was left behind. You could tell by the look on her face she had no clue she had been set up.

LYALL We'd almost forgotten about Barry when one day Mum told us he was coming to visit. He turned up in his Kombi van with his dog, possum traps, tobacco and a wry smile.

Barry slept in the van halfway up the drive. Al and I brought him cups of tea in the morning. There was love toward him but it had faded. We looked at Barry as though we were looking at a once favourite painting, or hearing an old song.

Not long after that - I must have been seven or so - Barry stopped outside the school. He waved me over. I was standing with Al, waiting for the bus home.

'Hello, Lyall, how are you?'

He seemed different. The real him? Sincere? Not the same him that chortled and chimed.

'Hey, mate, how are things at home? The thing is, mate . . . I want you to come and live with me.'

The woman next to him looked sheepish but smiled, projecting warmth towards me.

'Nah, I don't want to leave Al and Mum. Love you, see ya!'

And that's how I've handled tricky situations ever since.

Just when I thought I might be able to forget about Barry, Mum put me on a bus down to Ōpōtiki to go and visit him.

'Yeah, g'day, mate. How are you?' Barry said when I got off the bus. He had on his classic hat with a belt on it, a rollie hanging out his mouth. It was hot, and he wore a singlet, shorts and bare feet.

We didn't hug and, for some reason, I was a bit angry at him.

I tried not to show it as he introduced me to his dog, which he was taking to the vet.

'Hey, while I'm away, could you bring the ute up?' he asked when we got to the vet's. He spoke funny, different to the surfers, my new dad and his friends.

I was determined to show Barry I was a big kid now and that driving the ute up didn't faze me. I knew about the handbrake because a couple of times Al and I had been left in the car on a hill when the handbrake wasn't on enough. Al had yanked it up and we were okay. The other time, I steered the van away from parked cars and stopped it myself.

'We looked at Barry as though we were looking at a once favourite painting, or hearing an old song.'

I took the park brake off and turned the key. The ute jerked forward, so I kept doing it until I'd reached the front of the vet's.

'Good on ya, mate . . . you know how to drive?'

I could feel loving approval and broke into a smile.

'Whatever. Nah. My new dad lets us steer the wheel sometimes, but yeah . . .'

'You can drive home then, when we get to the gravel. You wanna smoke?'

'Yep.'

'Here, roll it yourself then. Roll me one, too.'

I rolled two crooked, loose smokes and we drove in silence as I spun out from the tobacco.

Pretty soon, I was back on the bus heading home to Auckland - ample time to get lost again between my two worlds.

HARRY Barry once wrote Mum a letter inviting us both down to Hokitika for a holiday. He said he'd got me a leather jacket. Mum suggested it might be a good idea for me to spend time with my father, but I was mainly interested in the leather jacket.

I must have been thirteen by this stage. We flew into Hokitika on a small plane. Once we had landed and collected our bags, we walked out of the tiny terminal and Barry was nowhere to be seen . . . until he casually walked out from behind a pillar in the car park. I found it very funny - I find it funny to this day. It's the kind of gentle humour he was capable of.

We piled into a clapped-out old truck and drove to Barry's mate Des's place. Des lived opposite a pub.

Mum got into a bad mood. I could never do much about it when she did that. I was grumpy myself because we had to stay somewhere else for the night and I wouldn't get my leather jacket until the next day.

Des had to talk by putting a buzzing machine on his throat, which had a hole in it, covered with a scarf. Sometimes the scarf would slip off and you could see the hole. It was a bit confusing at first, but didn't really bother me.

Des took me into his shed and said I could have a go with his air rifle. Then the grown-ups went across the road to the pub, which was supposed to be closed because it was Sunday, but there were a lot of cars in the car park. I used Des's clothesline for my target practice until there were no pegs left, then went to the pub to ask Des if he had any more pegs.

By the time I went in, everyone in the bar was being shuffled into the guest rooms and we had to sit quietly because the police had arrived. I'm guessing now that the pub being open on that Sunday was something to do with the fame of my father.

I remember seeing the police cars from a second-storey window. I remember Des being quietly mad at me for some reason. As an adult, I understand why he couldn't raise his voice, and what he was mad about, and that pegs are for hanging up washing, not shooting.

We bundled ourselves into the truck to go further south on an overnight drive. I pretended to be asleep for some of it - when I was presumed asleep, I got more information.

My father and mother talked of esoteric and philosophic things, including - and I remember this clearly - whether trucks/vehicles had a soul. They talked about writing, and lies, and if memory and truth are the same. Mum, as usual, spouted poetry, which sounded nice with the rattling of the old truck, and my father joined in when he knew the verses. For that time, I felt I had a mum and dad.

The morning brought us to a rotting house. Barry had a line of possum traps in the bush surrounding it. The property was an abandoned farm.

The leather jacket I'd been promised turned out to be a crocheted cardigan with suede patches. He'd found it at the local dump. For some reason, I wasn't disappointed.

We headed off for our own dump trip the next day, too - a half acre of rubbish full of promise. Nothing else mattered. All three of us were keen on sorting through stinky rubbish. We called out phrases like 'Look at this pile', 'Why did they get rid of that?' and 'No, Harry, we can't fit that on the truck, and anyway, it's buggered'. It was almost as though we were a family.

The next morning didn't go nearly as well. My father proudly announced that he and I were going to check the traps. If he thought it was some sort of bonding session, he was wrong. I was in teenage mode. I was a city boy and a vegetarian. Not that he planned to eat the poor animals.

'Mum, as usual, spouted poetry, which sounded nice with the rattling of the old truck, and my father joined in when he knew the verses. For that time, I felt I had a mum and dad.'

I clambered through the bush after him, bored out of my mind. I constantly complained about the cold, feeling odd in my women's cardigan, hoping to God he hadn't caught any possums. Thankfully, he hadn't. Maybe my whining scared them away.

My last memory of that time was Barry and my mother

arguing about whether they needed one or two sleeping bags in that creaking old house.

The truck turned up out of nowhere and out of no time. I would have been pushing sixteen by this stage and was still besotted by this towering man who smelled like leather. He told me never to smoke cigarettes or drink Johnny Walker whisky, like he did. 'Do as I say, not as I do' – I can say from first-hand experience that that maxim doesn't work.

I asked him to look at my chest muscles.

'They look just the same as a Cook Strait groper,' he said.

'Is that good or bad?' I asked.

'It's good . . . good for sliding under doors.'

Yes, it was funny at the time. Not only was I enamoured at the thought of a dad, he was very bright and funny. The knowledge that he was my father was a magic thought.

I'm not sure what I expected then, but I know now that all I hoped for was time – time to be with him and learn something.

Subsequently, I've learned that a benign presence is the basis of healthy attachment. It's less important how rich, clever or whatever else we are. If we stay beside someone with love, they will grow well, even with our mistakes. Abandonment is the most intense way of being unloved.

That day we had the 'life, the universe and everything in between' conversation. We started out on a walk from Aro Street to Willis Street, on a quest for hamburgers from Wimpy, one of my favourite joints, and a five- to six-kilometre round trip. He told me he would never be a father (let alone a good one), how to navigate the bush (by following ridges), and how to blow your nose without a handkerchief, which I was a little bit shocked by.

This was the first of a few visits he made to Mum – almost

Barry, Te Teko, 1968.

annually. He stopped visiting around the time I became what he might have wanted - a man.

MARTIN Barry married his third wife, Vanda, in 1969. She, like the rest of us, was sucked into Barry's world by being told everything she wanted to hear and more.

They moved to the small North Island town of Te Teko, where Barry would meet good friend George Johnson. Then later that year, something so terrible happened that it would shatter Barry's world and stun a nation.

The idea of an adventure camp for young men was a good one and should have been a runaway success, but that's not how it turned out. A group of businessmen came up with the idea. They formed a company and promptly put Barry Crump, the great Kiwi bushman, and his mate George in charge of running it.

The camp was set up in a remote and rugged area inland from Whakatāne. You stayed at the camp for a week and the cost was forty dollars.

Also around this time, Barry Crump Knives came out. They were well made and of good quality, and came with a leather sheath with Barry's name stitched into the side.

I was ten years old, my brother Ivan was eleven. The perks of being the sons of the Good Keen Man meant we were able to spend a week of the August school holidays at the camp. I went first and Ivan came down for the second week, so we were not together. I don't know why. It probably would have been too much for Barry anyway.

With my bag packed, Mum put me on the bus in Auckland and I was on my way.

I was excited about the camp. I didn't know what to expect. I was also a little excited about seeing my father, as I'd only met him for the first time the year before, on my birthday.

I met Barry again at the end of my bus journey. He and George bundled me into the back of a Land Rover and we set off for the camp, Barry and George talking and smoking rollies along the way - they were both such brilliant storytellers.

It has been over fifty years since that drive to the camp and I have never forgotten it. We ran out of tar-sealed road as we neared Lake Matahina; the gravel road was potholed and narrow. The lake was to the right, with a sheer drop of more than ten metres in places straight down to the water below, with no guard rail or safety fence. And there was a bank on the left, so nowhere to bail out.

'Later that year, something so terrible happened that it would shatter Barry's world and stun a nation.'

I hid behind the seat, terrified we were going to bounce off the track straight into the lake below. I would peek over the seat now and then and see the bush line in the distance, hoping to make it out alive.

Barry sensed my fear, which he found amusing. He just carried on driving at the same breakneck speed. I moved to lie down on the floor of the Land Rover, to stop being thrown about. As it would turn out, my fear was justified.

With huge relief, we made it to the camp. It was pretty basic:

a few hand-built cabins, no showers or bath. When I got off the bus in Auckland a week later, Mum said she could smell me from quite a distance. The toilet was a large pit in the ground with two posts across it; you straddled the posts and went to the toilet in between them. No one said anything about it, so neither did I . . . but a long drop would have been markedly better.

There were bunks in the cabins, with a pillow and a couple of blankets provided, as it was winter. I remember the cold.

I was treated well, which may have been because of who my father was. I still received a couple of clips around the ears from the older boys but that was well deserved – I could be cheeky.

In the week I was there, Barry and George turned up at the camp only three or four times, for a few hours. They did not stay at the camp at night. They were probably propping up a bar somewhere in town.

There was a leader in our camp when Barry and George were gone, a fifteen-year-old fella named Gary. Barry put me in his care for the week. Gary was quite remarkable for his age: brought up in the country, he had no licence but could drive anything. He could hunt, shoot, gut, fence, build, mend, fix and lead, and everyone respected and thought highly of Gary. He was confident without being full of himself, so he was very well liked.

What was to happen in just over a week's time would be catastrophic for Gary – and not of his making. I have never seen him since. I hope he is doing well these days.

No one had caught or seen a pig for the first two days I was there. A hunting party would consist of about eight young men, with one person to head the hunt, but there was nothing about, so we ate a lot of damper. These were made of flour, salt, milk, butter and sugar, then cooked over an open fire – they were great with jam, but that soon ran out. I was also treated to my first feed of huhu grubs - big fat wriggly things pulled out of a rotten log in the bush. These they cooked up on the fire in a pan or on the end of a shovel. Once cooked, the grub's head would go dark - you would hold this bit while you ate the body. I was a ten-year-old city boy, and at first this seemed disgusting to look at, let alone eat, but to my surprise I actually enjoyed them; I thought they tasted like peanut butter and went looking for more.

The next day, Barry turned up and took a group of us out for a hunt. We were all excited that he was actually spending time with us. We weren't gone long before everyone took off in different directions, chasing squealing and grunting pigs through the bush.

Suddenly, Barry appeared and handed me a tiny piglet, saying, 'Stay here, hold this,' before disappearing again. The piglet was beside itself, wriggling and squirming in my arms and squealing so loud. I was standing all alone in the bush with it; we were both frightened. I know I was told not to let the piglet go, but after what felt like such a long time, I did just that. The poor little thing just wanted its mother. I think I did, too.

The next thing, I heard yelling in the distance, followed by quiet. Triumphantly, our hunting party eventually appeared on the track, Barry at the lead, with four of them carrying a huge wild boar tied to a branch, the rest carrying knives and rifles. I can picture now the smiles on all their faces as we marched into the camp with the magnificent bounty.

They strung the pig up and gutted it. I couldn't believe what I saw. They buried the guts, then built a fire under the pig, singeing and burning all of the hair off it, then used the back of a knife to scrape the carcass clean. A group of boys kept the fire going, turning the pig for many hours till just after dark. Then in groups we carved strips of meat off for our dinner.

What a day. That night, in our bunks, the stories of hunting and catching the man-eating beast grew and grew. By the time sleep came, the marauding black boar was the size of an elephant.

During the day, there was target practice with the rifles - they had set up a range. I loved it, and it turned out I wasn't a bad shot, either. To their credit, they taught us how to carry a gun, load it, unload it, fire it, climb a fence with it, where and how to point it when walking through the bush - all good skills.

The nights were the most fun. We all sat around the campfire telling stories and jokes. As I was so young, I mostly listened, but this sure was living. I certainly grew up some in my time at the camp.

My week came to an end, and the trip back into town to meet the bus wasn't so terrifying. Perhaps I'd hardened up.

When back in Auckland, I was thrown in the bath and my clothes were washed twice. It took Mum some time to stop me swearing in every sentence I spoke - she was pretty good about it. She understood I'd been with older boys. It was now my brother Ivan's turn for his week at the camp.

As with me, Ivan was spending a lot of the time with Gary. One afternoon, there were two groups out on a hunt at the far end of the lake. They had a good day and decided to have a couple of beers. As I recall it, remembering that Ivan was only eleven years old, Barry pulled him out of the back of Gary's Land Rover and took him back to camp with his group.

Not long after that, Gary started to head back with his group. Tragically, he hit a rough patch on the road and the Land Rover rolled down the bank into the deep and dark lake below. Gary and the other young men in the front seat managed to get out and make for the surface. But the back door of the Land Rover was broken some time before the accident I think, so the five boys in the back could not get out that way. One of them trapped in the back tried to get to the front of the Land Rover, but got his clothing caught on the interior window. Gary and the other young men dived down several times each but could not save their mates. All five boys drowned that day.

The camp was shut down immediately. Police investigations followed, with Barry and George put up on charges of manslaughter. Ultimately, the charges were dropped.

The public was not happy about that, and who could blame them? There was negligence and carelessness on a grand scale, this was obvious. I'd seen it first-hand myself the week before. What of the company behind it all? I don't know if the directors had to answer to any charges, though they did play a role in it.

The families of those boys - I don't believe they got any answers.

In later years, I spoke to Barry about it. He went very quiet and said little. I know it weighed heavily on him. I'll let you be the judge of whether Barry and George should have done time, but I believe their real penalty was living with what happened. Five young men died in their care. It must affect you somehow.

Barry became a member of the Bahá'í faith a few years later and remained one for the rest of his life.

As for the camp, young men living rough, learning to shoot, hunt, fish and other outdoor skills is still a great idea in my opinion.

I'm grateful Ivan was pulled from the back of the Land Rover that fateful afternoon.

IVAN I know that when those five boys drowned at the camp under Barry's care, he was deeply upset and not primarily about himself. I was there. All the criticisms were basically true.

It was an accident, a tragic event due to no one noticing the

Playing croquet in Waihī.
Left to right: Ruby, Barry
and Martin.

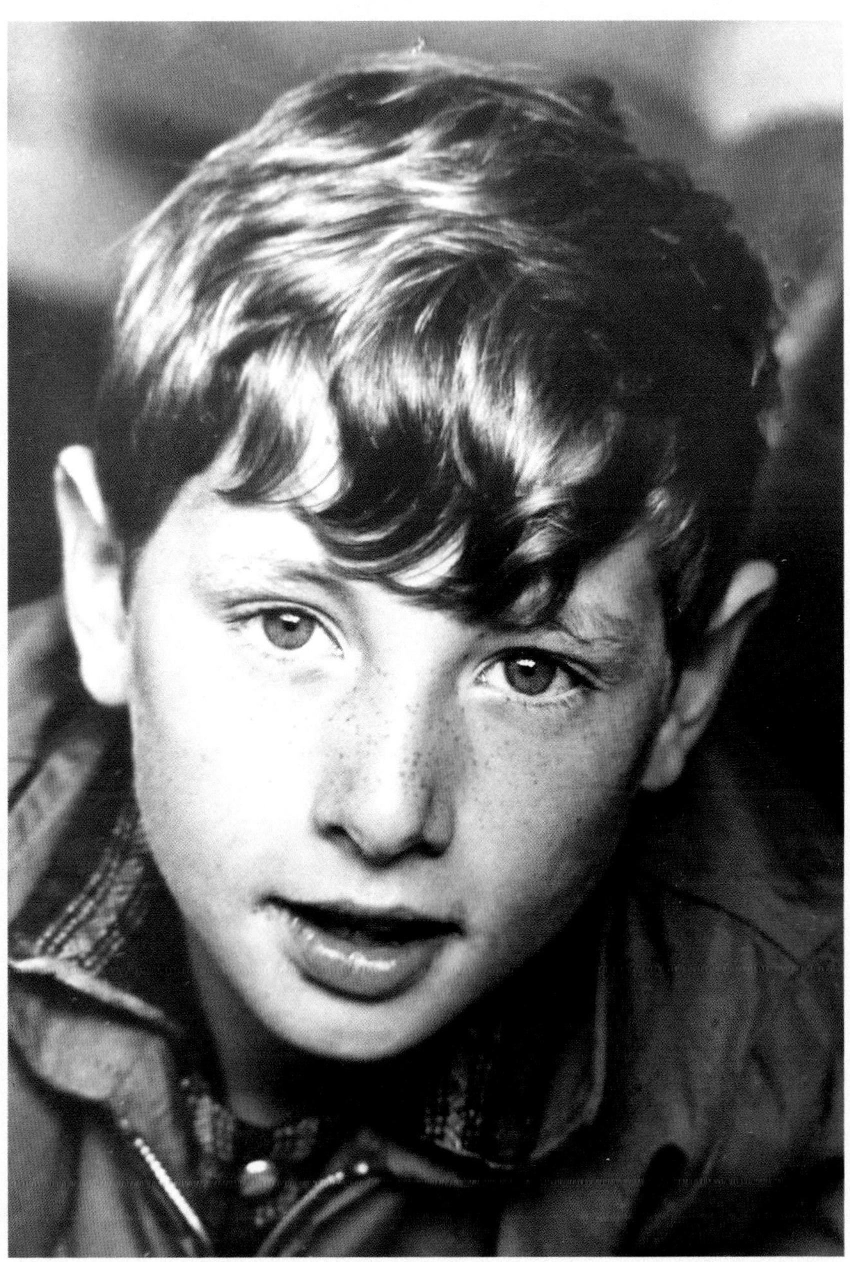

A young Martin.

Top Lyall (left) and his brother Alan on a quiet street, Spain, 1972.

Above Lyall (right), Alan and their mum Vanda free camping in Germany, 1972.

Barry, Lyall (being held) and
Alan in the dope fields of
Ketama, Morocco, 1972.

Martin calls Barry 'Dad', a joke worthy of a good laugh.

Ivan and Barry at Astley Avenue during a rendition of 'The Ballad of Eskimo Nell'.

A publicity shot for the release of *Bastards I Have Met*, 1971.

Barry wanders up the Pakihi River with a carton of his new book *Bullock Creek*, 1989.

Barry, 1994, just a couple of years before his death.

back-door lever had been broken off. There were two vehicles going out hunting that night. I had the choice, so I went with Barry. Lucky for me. Gary dived down at least three times to try to save the boys. The last time he couldn't reach the Land Rover because it had slipped further down. I felt very sorry for Gary. I liked him.

> **'I know that when those five boys drowned at the camp under Barry's care, he was deeply upset and not primarily about himself.'**

MARTIN It must have been tough on Vanda, as I know she was copping it hard from Barry and his ever-changing moods, especially at this time. I've no doubt she copped it from the public fallout from the camp as well.

Some time later, Barry and Vanda bought a property in Waihī, which for Barry was putting down roots, something he didn't do often.

Mum took my grandmother Ruby, Ivan and me for a visit. Vanda was very welcoming and friendly. I remember the croquet lawn they had. It looked like a professional set-up. There were a couple of places around the lawn where Barry had whisky stashed. He would stop at every opportunity and have a drink.

After that, I wouldn't see Barry for another four years.

I was growing up large and fast. At thirteen, I was pinching Mum's cigarettes and sneaking around and hiding to smoke them. When she caught me under the house with cigarettes and matches, she was too worried I'd set the place on fire, so from that day, I smoked with Mum and Wally in the house.

Ivan had talked Mum into growing marijuana in the vegetable garden. She was an excellent gardener - the plants grew big and healthy.

It was 1974. I loved music and was an especially big fan of Elton John. On a hot February night at Western Springs, Elton was on the *Goodbye Yellow Brick Road* tour. The album had just been released. I had the album and a ticket for the concert - it was the best.

Over 40,000 of us witnessed the incredible concert. Coloured smoke rose out of Elton's piano while he played 'Funeral for a Friend', then he jumped up in a chicken suit and just smashed the song 'Love Lies Bleeding'. He performed the entire album and sent us all home with an encore of 'Crocodile Rock'. I'm still a fan to this day. I've now seen him live four times.

It was a night I will never forget. What I found out many years later is that Barry was in the crowd that night, too. It's a shame we weren't together.

LYALL I sometimes think about the things I said to Barry as a teen. I called him by his name rather than Dad, hardly spoke to him, never hugged him and said 'whatever' a lot.

'You like that word, don't you?' he said back to me once.

Mum decided I needed to see Barry again, and this time I could bring my two friends.

I showed off. It was 1981 and Barry was a bestselling author, on telly all the time and loved and admired by most of New Zealand. He got us to clear the possums from the traps, feed the pigs and gather firewood. He even asked if I could help him with his latest novel.

I started calling him Dad again. He took us hunting, let us shoot the big gun and we washed naked in the stream. Then we were back on the bus to Auckland. I had a pocket full of money and bought myself a bowie knife. I wanted to be just like my old dad, Barry.

I felt lost again when we arrived that night at the bus station in Auckland. Mum was supposed to pick us up but Barry was meant to have rung Mum and let her know we had caught the bus. We had to beg for money to catch a bus to my mate's grandparents in Point Chev.

My mate bragged to a stranger that we had just been staying with Barry Crump and that I was his son.

The novelty had worn off by that stage, though. I just wanted to get back to my real family and Mum's great cooking.

Barry, Lyall (riding up front)
and his brother Alan, 1972.

5.

Broken Idols

Getting to know the real Barry

‘I silently thanked Mum for getting away from this scary man, my father.’

MARTIN We could see what Barry was up to by simply reading the papers. One of these wild adventures took him off overseas to find God.

Barry, Vanda, Lyall and Alan headed for England and Germany, where Barry abandoned them, I think to Vanda's relief, even though she was penniless and a long way from home. They had all suffered enough.

Barry bought a motorbike and travelled all the way to Kashmir on the border of Pakistan and India. There, he stayed with a young Indian fella named Sheffey and his family.

By now, Barry was deep in his spiritual quest. I don't know for sure if the five boys drowning at the camp had any bearing on this, but I suspect it did.

He was there for several months, until it was time to make his way back to New Zealand. Back home, he found himself driving along the Desert Road and stopped to pick up a hitchhiker. This guy, for some reason, left a book on the Bahá'í faith in Barry's van. In it, Barry found what he had been looking for and became a Bahá'í – and remained one for the rest of his life.

It must have been about 1988. I was busy at home trying to fix something – I'll be the first to admit that I'm not much of a handyman – when the phone rang. I answered quite abruptly: 'Yes?'

'Hello there, this is Newstalk ZB with the cashbox call. How are you today?'

I then realised I was on the air. I said, 'I'm okay, thank you.'

'Who are we speaking to?'

'Martin.'

'Martin who?

Here we go . . .

'Martin Crump.'

'Oh, are you related to the famous Barry Crump?'

I couldn't be bothered making up a lie, so I declared that yes, I was his son. We talked for a minute or so. The host asked what I did and where I worked. I told him. We finally got around to the money in the cashbox. It was $476 and I had to guess how many cents. I got it wrong and hung up. I thought nothing more about it.

I was at work in the kitchen a week or so later when I noticed this old bloke standing in the doorway, staring at me. He called out, 'I was listening to the radio the other day. That's how I tracked you down. So you're Martin? I'm your grandfather,' and he came and shook my hand. His hand was huge and strong, even if it belonged to an old man.

This was Wally, not to be confused with my stepfather Wally. This was my grandfather Wally, Barry's father. All Barry had ever said about him was that he was a hard old man.

I invited him in to sit down. He had his partner, Joyce, with him. We talked for some time. They seemed a very pleasant older couple.

I looked at Wally. He had a square jaw and his face was hard and lined. I'd have guessed that he'd been a tough fella in his time.

I was to find out just how hard he was. And it would shock everyone.

Wally Crump – the boys' grandfather
– and his partner, Joyce.

Now he got around with a walking stick and had Meals on Wheels delivered to him, which he couldn't stand.

Over the next two or more years, I would cook meals for Wally and Joyce. I'd send them off with full plates at least twice a week. They brought back the empty ones. I didn't charge them; they were family.

I got to know them better over this time, of course. Wally loved to tell stories. I could tell that he lived a lot off Barry's success as a writer.

One day, with great fanfare, Wally brought in a book that he had written himself titled *McDunnit Dunnit*, and signed it for me. I must say, I quite enjoyed it. He can tell a story.

I left that catering contract and lost touch with them after that, but I did keep them well fed for a time.

When I next caught up with Barry, I told him about Wally and the book that he had written and given me. Barry said he was highly embarrassed that his father had written a book and wished he hadn't.

It was several months later when Mum rang me and said that Barry needed my help. I was to meet him at Mum's at 7pm. I was on time. He wasn't.

When he did turn up, it was all hush-hush as he hurried me out the door, asking me to drive him all the way out to Waiuku. It turned out it was just so he could pick up some dope to smoke, from someone he barely knew. It all sounded dodgy to me.

I was driving, we were talking away, while Barry rolled a joint in the car and we smoked it. We left the windows up, so we made a good stew.

Wow, I was very stoned. I could see why he wanted more of this smoke.

By now, we were right out in the country and it felt like we'd been driving for days. No streetlights and it was pitch black.

I was sure we were lost when Barry happened to ask, 'Where are we?'

In my stupor, I said, 'We're just going past here.'

We both burst out laughing. Neither of us knew where here was, and we laughed until we were crying. I had to stop driving. I was going to wet my pants. I'm not sure that Barry didn't. We laughed until our faces ached.

We never did find the place we were looking for, or the bloke. We should never have had that smoke - it sure was funny, though.

I do consider myself very fortunate to be living in the time I was, to find myself in the company of such great talent. Bryce Peterson, Barry's old mate, had a flat in town. By good fortune, I was hanging out with him one time when Barry turned up with his good friends, performing artists Paul Bennett and Linda Poulton. They arrived unannounced. The drinks quickly went from tea to whisky.

They could all play guitar, and Linda, Paul and Bryce can sing. I'd been around these people many times before, and, rather than ask them to play and sing for me, I strategically left the guitar leaning against an arm on the sofa. This way, they would pick it up when they were ready, and you'd get the best of them.

It wasn't long before Paul picked up the guitar and Linda started singing. I was in heaven with a free ticket to the show. It was at this gathering that I learned about the bottle saxophone. Bryce got an empty wine bottle, soaked a piece of string with lighter fluid, wrapped the string around the neck of the bottle and lit it, then broke the bottle cleanly where the string was lit. Then he pulled the gold foil out of a cigarette packet, which was folded over and placed above the wine bottle top. Bryce blew through the paper into the bottle. It really did sound like a

Left to right: Martin, Barry, unidentified friend and Bryce Peterson, sitting in front of the hut on Bill Moller's farm.

saxophone. What a party we had that afternoon - out of nothing came something so wonderful. What talent, what fun.

STEPHEN I always knew I was adopted. I was fortunate that the family who took me in were good people so, for that reason mostly, I'd never thought too much about my biological parents.

I was thirty years old, married with two children and getting on with life when, out of nowhere, this adoption agency contacted me asking me to call them. I wasn't sure at first, but at the insistence of my wife, Leigh, I did. If I'm being honest, I was also by then a little curious to know about this part of my past.

They informed me that my birth mother wanted to talk to me. I discovered her name was Jean Watson. The first thing she told me was that my father was Barry Crump.

Naturally, I was surprised. I'd read a few of his books - I liked them and I thought he was cool, so to find out he was my father was pretty interesting, to say the least. Jean went on to tell me that I have a full brother named Harry, younger than me, who was also adopted out. This was all quite a bit to take in, as you might appreciate.

Thereafter, I rarely ever mentioned who my father was, even to close friends - it's not my way. But a few people found out and reckoned I look a bit like him.

It would have been not much longer than a year after this revelation that I was in Christchurch with a friend and saw a red Toyota ute parked outside a pub. We had a bit of a joke with each other - imagine if that's Barry Crump's. Then we see him in the pub . . . the ute *is* his.

Instantly, I felt nervous, but my mate nudged me forward and encouraged me to say hi to him. He pointed out that I might not get the chance again.

As I walked towards Barry, I thought he was just as you'd expect – in a Swanndri and boots; I could smell the bush on him. He was smoking a large roll-your-own cigarette, and drinking Elephant beer with whisky chasers – and this was during the day.

It was a bit surreal seeing my father for the first time. It was almost as if he had just walked straight out of a Sam Cash novel.

He looked at me and, somehow, immediately knew exactly who I was – his third son (after Ivan and Martin), his first from Jean Watson.

'It was a bit surreal seeing my father for the first time. It was almost as if he had just walked straight out of a Sam Cash novel.'

He had a knockabout bloke with him. 'Are you a son, too?' I asked.

'No,' he replied, 'just a mate.'

Barry and I talked for about twenty minutes, nothing too deep, no animosity. The meeting was friendly enough. He wished me well and a good life.

I'm glad I did speak to him because, as it turned out, my friend was right – I never did get the chance again.

I've now had a good many years to digest all of this, and I can honestly say I have no criticism or resentment of my birth parents at all. Jean was very arty, bohemian - that's fine, but just not for me. And as for Barry - well, he shot through, so there's nothing to miss there. I've gotta say I'm okay with my lot. I've had mentors and good people around me all my life to fill in any gaps - many don't have that.

IVAN I was once talking to Barry about tattoos. He reckoned he would have been black with them if he had ever started, but every time he left the pub, the tattoo shop was closed and he was broke by then anyway because, as always, alcohol came first.

He did have words of wisdom, though, some of which have stuck with me. Barry and I were one day yarning about love, and he said he reckoned love is caring.

'If you want to learn to love, get a dog. If you want to learn how to fight, get married. If you want to be happy, grow a garden.'

This is from his mouth, through my ears, and to your eyes. Try and fault that.

MARTIN It was 1977 and Barry was back to get his dose of the city life. He had this idea to travel around the country on motorbikes, to take all the side roads you would normally drive past and see who or what was there.

He went to Blue Wing Honda and pitched his idea to them - not only did they go for it, they handed him three motorbikes. TV said they liked the idea as well and to let them know when he found someone or something of interest and they would send the film crew.

Barry got the 750CC, his girlfriend Margo got the smaller

Bill Moller.

125CC, and his good mate Bryce got the XL250CC trail bike.

As for a place to stay, Mum and Barry had a mutual friend, Bill Moller, who owned a large bush block property in Oratia, in West Auckland. Bill was a local identity and would hold the Auckland folk festivals at his place. They were legendary. He had a large barn made out of demolition timber with a huge fireplace, and room for everyone. It was very rustic, with great atmosphere.

Barry chose a little valley, right at the back of Bill's property, to hang his hat. They decided to build Barry a hut there and wasted no time getting on with it. As luck would have it, this was when I turned up, just in time to help. I was eighteen and working with Wally in the family catering business, which gave me three or four days a week off to help with the build.

Another stroke of luck came my way. Bryce was pulled away to go on tour with a friend performing his children's songs at schools around the South Island, so I was handed the XL250 - and the fun began.

Barry was very relaxed and at peace for some reason, which made this time together all the more enjoyable. In a few short weeks, the hut was finished. We must have built it all right because it was still standing many years later.

Before we knew it, a television crew was interviewing Barry on the steps of our newly built hut, which he took most of the credit for building. He told a reporter about the clean life he was now living, and how at peace with the world he was, all because of his Bahá'í faith. No alcohol or drugs, no sleeping with women.

Barry had just told the reporter a whole load of porkies. He was still doing those things, if in a much more measured way - not to the excess like he had in the past.

Margo was a very cool lady who had been a Bahá'í longer than Barry had and was teaching him. If I was ever there at night around the campfire, the conversation would always turn back to the Bahá'í teachings. Because I'd helped build the hut, I felt it gave me a little more freedom to drop by and visit. Occasionally, I'd bring a friend to meet Barry, but I was very selective about who I took.

Only once did we ever use the bikes for what they had been intended, but we'd found nothing worth bringing a film crew in for. On another occasion later on, Barry did ride north and, up one of those side roads, he found an old chap with the most interesting past and story. You couldn't see much of his face - just white hair everywhere. His house was as untidy as he was. Barry contacted the film crew and three days later they still hadn't turned up. The moment was gone. That's what Barry would often say he really didn't like about television - it was too slow.

New Zealand later had a very popular TV series called *Heartland*, a great show that enabled us to watch ourselves in our own homes and towns. Barry's idea had been about doing just that, but he just never had the patience to see it through - a shame, as it could have been really terrific.

I had that Honda XL250 for three or four months, until Bryce came back from his tour. He had the bike for only a couple of weeks before he had an accident and wrecked it. That marked the end of Barry's TV series idea, but I'd had a great time while it lasted.

During this time with Barry, I was seeing him through older eyes. I noticed how every time we were in a shop, takeaway or anywhere that had a till, Barry was incredibly slow to get his wallet out. I paid for most things. In fact, I don't remember him paying for anything at any time. The great Kiwi bushman was mean with his money - something I had not inherited. Money and me were enemies - I was always giving the stuff away.

I also saw a playful side of him. Out of the blue one night, as I was about to head home on the bike, Barry told me he desperately needed my motorcycle helmet for a good friend who was arriving the next day from overseas and that he had to pick up from the airport. He promised to return it to me afterwards. He then handed me some sort of helmet to ride home with. It was like a prop from an old movie, something Biggles would have worn decades years ago. I looked bloody ridiculous, and I was highly embarrassed - I was 18 and this was not a cool look.

I was very pleased it was night time as I reluctantly put the helmet on. I rode home the back way, and I wasn't mucking about. I came to the first set of lights when I heard a big commotion behind me. It was Barry and Margo, pointing and laughing and beeping the horns on their motorbikes. They brought the most attention to my humiliation. He had set me up, the bugger. Their ridicule continued at every set of lights, hooting, tooting and laughing all the way home to my place, where Barry handed me back my helmet and we all laughed.

Barry had been in the hut at Bill's for several months and was starting to think of going bush again. He had had his eye on a Model A truck for a while but didn't have the $3000 needed to buy it. This is where Barry used his patience.

'I don't know where from,' he said, 'but somehow the money I need will come.'

So, he waited and waited and eventually, inexplicably, the money did come. He bought the cool-looking Model A truck and, once again, he left the city life behind.

I look back at this time with fondness - of those fireside nights at the hut where Barry would share a softer, gentler side of himself, and a spiritual side I'd not seen in my father before. He was calm and, as much as he could be, at peace.

It would be a few years before we would meet again but then we would spend a year together.

Barry stands at the front of the hut Martin helped him build.

Barry made it all the way south to Wānaka in the Model A (by himself, after splitting with Margo), and there he settled down for a while. I believe this is where he met Robin, who would become his fourth wife. They would stay together for the next twelve years - the longest relationship he ever had with a partner or wife.

Barry wrote a ripping yarn, *Gold and Greenstone*, around this time. A great story and book, in my opinion.

Barry and Robin next headed to Moke Lake, just out of Queenstown, on a whole new adventure. They moved into an abandoned shack in a place called Zephyr Town. They would gold prospect and mine here for the next two years. My uncle Bill, Barry's older brother, joined them.

Barry got totally carried away with a decent dose of gold fever. The biggest nugget Barry and Robin found they gave to their bank manager, as he'd helped them through some lean times. It was freezing cold in winter and very isolated. They did well to last two years. Then they made their way north to thaw out.

It has to be said some of the books Barry wrote were absolute gems - a couple of these, as we know, were to become Kiwi classics. Then, on the other hand, quite a number of them were written to keep food on the table and diesel in the truck.

In 1980, Barry's latest offering was one of these: not at all destined to become a classic, but one I enjoyed for a few reasons. The book is called *Shorty*, and it's about a farmer short in stature. But you'd be careful never to go on about his height or you'd end up receiving a long tirade of abuse from Shorty, who had an excellent grasp of the English language. Shorty would fall in love with the game of golf and develop golf fever bad.

The timing of me picking up and reading *Shorty* was uncanny, as I had just started playing golf again and had joined the beautiful Waitākere Golf Club. What happened next all happened very quickly and fell so easily into place.

Barry turned up one day, unannounced, in a VW van with Robin - this was the first time I met her. The whole vibe was very hippie. I liked it, being a bit of a hippie myself.

'I look back at this time with fondness – of those fireside nights at the hut where Barry would share a softer, gentler side of himself, and a spiritual side I'd not seen in my father before.'

I said to Barry, 'I've just read *Shorty* and as you've just written a book on golf you really should come and have a look at my new golf club up in the Waitākere Ranges.'

To my surprise, he was dead keen and told me to lead the way. I jumped in my car, while Barry and Robin followed in the van.

It's quite a spectacular sight, laying eyes on the Waitākere Golf Club for the first time. You drive through a wooded area, up the hill and, as you come over the rise, there it is. It's hard to believe - to stand there on the beautiful grounds, surrounded by pristine native bush with the Cascade Stream and waterfalls running along its boundary, and still only be a half hour's drive away from Queen Street in downtown Auckland.

I showed them around, and the more Barry saw, the more he liked. What sealed it was the recent wild-pig tracks across the sixteenth green. This was indeed Crump country. Barry and Robin needed a place to stay, and here it was.

A deal was struck with the committee of the golf club - Barry and Robin could stay on the course (sleeping in their trusty VW van), use the showers and bathroom facilities, and play golf. In return, Barry would write a piece for the club's monthly newsletter. They would have the well-known Barry Crump as a member, who would also provide some security for the isolated property. Win-win.

I was still in the family catering business, and my work days were Wednesdays through Saturdays. We decided on playing golf on Mondays and Tuesdays to avoid the weekends - neither of us liked crowds.

It all felt natural as we settled into a routine on that first Monday morning. I turned up at 8am and we teed off on the first hole. Barry was a pretty handy golfer but as I'd played a lot more, we never played each other - we only played against ourselves to better our last score. We liked it that way. Besides, neither of us had an official handicap.

We finished our first round of golf together and Barry got a good look around his new home and grounds.

Robin had the billy boiling for a much-needed mug of tea, along with a stack of sandwiches. We merrily consumed all this while we analysed and discussed how we could improve on our scores. Barry suggested we go again, so we did.

We played two rounds on that first day, which was to become

the norm. Two rounds on Mondays and Tuesdays. Our games would improve quite quickly at this rate, and so would our fitness. The Waitākere course is set in the hills, where a flat lie is hard to find.

I must also mention how much I appreciated Robin standing back and allowing me to have this time with my father. Not once, not ever, did she make me feel like I was taking up their time together. She might just have enjoyed some time to herself.

It wasn't long before the word was out - Barry Crump was the newest member of Waitākere Golf Club. Most were very good and gave us plenty of elbow room. It was usually just Barry and me on the course, as early in the week meant it was pretty empty. We loved it that way.

On a rare occasion, I would bring a friend - Kevin, a handy golfer himself. I had to be very selective about who I brought into the circle as we didn't need anyone gushing over Barry and not being themselves. This would have spoiled the day and made me look like a plonker. Kevin was cool, so he could join us.

The news that Barry was back in town had reached the attention of the formidable Gordon Dryden, who had just started a new radio station called Radio Pacific in Manukau. Barry, Robin and I went out there to meet him one day. Barry was offered the job of a radio host for a show called 'The Bush Telegraph', which would run Mondays through Fridays, from 5 to 7am. Robin was to be the producer. They were offered $500 a week, which they accepted on the spot.

It was perfect. I'd meet Barry on the first tee at 7.30am, as that's when he got back to the course after the radio show. I would never have imagined that in twenty-five years' time, I'd be sitting in the same seat at Radio Pacific, running my own show. Funny old world.

It was such a nice thing to see the look on Barry's face that told me he was genuinely pleased to see me - then we would tee off on the first for another day together.

It would be the usual fare of bush tea and sandwiches after the first round. Then, after all the post-mortems on our score, we'd head out again. We didn't always complete our second round, as fatigue sometimes took over - Barry was starting his day at around 3.30am, so it was understandable he'd get weary.

I could tell when Barry was getting tired because he'd get cheeky. He'd say 'nice shot' to me as I was on a downswing, before I'd even hit the ball. I'd usually burst out laughing. Then as he was on his downswing, ready to smash his ball down the fairway, I'd throw a golf ball at his ball and knock it off the tee, so he'd have his mad swipe at it and miss. This was the time to head back. Although we never did anything like this if one of us was scoring and playing well; if one of us had something going then we would see it out until the end.

One day during this time, a friend of mine on the committee at the golf club, who had been calculating our scores over the last few weeks, walked all the way across to the thirteenth hole and gave Barry and me our very first official handicaps. Barry got a fifteen, I got a seven. You couldn't crowbar the smile off Barry's face - mine too. This just made us keener.

I think it's fair to say that, just like in Barry's book *Shorty*, we both had golf fever. We were getting on so well, which makes what happened next so hard to understand.

Every now and again, we would test ourselves and play on another course. There are a number of great golf courses in our district, such as Helensville and South Head. The one we chose for this particular week was Muriwai, out at the beach on the rugged west coast - a beautiful course which, depending on the wind, could be very tough.

We were both excited about the day, and the weather was

glorious. Barry picked me up in his car and we teased each other all the way out there. As you'll remember, we never actually played against each other, but that didn't stop us from ribbing one another. I suggested that perhaps he might want to park the car close to the eighteenth green, so he could make a quick getaway after the game because it could be embarrassing, people seeing the great, tough Barry Crump sobbing like a baby after the hiding I was about to dish up. You know, that sort of thing.

With much excitement, we teed off in perfect conditions. We were both playing okay as we got through the first few holes. Then, as we made it to the first par-five, I drove my ball well up the fairway, so no problems. I got out my fairway wood and, in that moment, something I still struggle to explain came over me, from my toes to the top of my head. I felt myself go red. I could see very little as I felt a rage rising up through me. I hit that ball as hard as I could. I had no idea what direction it went. I pulled another ball out of my bag and hit it as hard as I could. Still, I couldn't see where it went. I must have hit about a dozen balls, behaving like an absolute madman.

I wonder what Barry was thinking. I walked up the fairway with my head down. I felt shattered, like I had just been through something devastating. I found one of the balls I'd hit and with one hand I knocked it up towards the green. We walked in absolute silence over the next few holes, then back to the clubhouse and our car. I was still just using one hand to hit the ball a few yards at a time. I was numb.

Barry broke the silence at last, as we approached the ninth green.

'What are you like at playing pool?'

I said I could hold my own. We loaded up the car and drove away in silence until we reached the Huapai Tavern, then went inside.

Barry was straight up to the bar and ordered us two beers with two whisky chasers, and a load of change for the pool table. We must have had seven or eight games of pool with as many beers and whisky chasers to match. I was getting very drunk and starting to stagger. I remember one or two people wanting to join us, but Barry insisted that this was a father and son grudge match, and that we had to see it through without interruption.

We were still playing and drinking when workers started dropping into the pub at the end of the day. I was still feeling anger, and I was knocking into them in my drunken stupor, eyeballing them, daring them to say or do anything. I felt like I could have torn the place apart.

The truth is I could have been pushed over by a nine-year-old kid, I was so wasted.

Then it was home time and Barry, the snake, sat me in the driver's seat. Yes, in my condition - he had a terrible fear of being caught drunk-driving but had no such fear of me being caught, obviously. He steered the car from the passenger seat while I somehow worked the pedals. We made it to my place. I didn't turn up for golf the next day, as I thought we could do with a breather. That, and I was feeling quite foolish.

The best I can come up with for my outburst is perhaps I was holding on to some sort of resentment about him not being around when I was younger - *Why couldn't it have been like this always?* - but I'm not even sure if that's the reason. I think back to how Barry guided me through this. He seemed to know what to do.

When I turned up the following Monday for our game, all was back to normal and we carried on.

There were many good reasons to play golf at Waitākere. One I liked in particular was that we never had to pay for golf balls. The perimeter of the course is lined with thick bush, so, of course, we lost golf balls but, also, we could find them when we needed them.

The eleventh hole is a short par-three with a large bank on the right-hand side covered with gorse about eight feet high – Barry had threatened on more than one occasion to go in there and see what he could find.

We played the first round on this Tuesday morning and both commented on how low on golf balls we'd got. So, Barry said today was the day. He put on a big heavy coat and gloves, with a sack over his shoulder. He disappeared into the gorse for about an hour. When he came out the other side he was covered with bracken, bits of gorse and sodden with sweat, but with the sack at least half full. When he tipped the sack open on the ground, we counted over 180 golf balls. Some were yellow with age, very old and unusable, but there were a heap of very playable balls that would last us for ages.

The closest Barry ever got to being affectionate was when he called me 'matey potata'. I didn't mind being a potata, especially a matey potata. Besides, he called a lot of people matey potata, and Robin, of course, was the number one matey potata, so I'm not getting carried away with myself. I just liked it.

I turned up to the golf course one morning and there was Robin, quite upset as Barry had told her another woman needed him more than Robin did. He had suggested she go and have a word with me. I had no clue who this other woman was or how Barry had any time to start anything. It was the first crack to appear in the eight or nine months they had been living at the golf club.

Then news came back that, not for the first time, Barry and Robin had been found in the shower together, with their washing

Barry enjoys a beer at the
Newmarket Hotel, 1972.

hanging up around the place, which the club's committee deemed to be a step too far. They had outstayed their welcome. Their time at Waitākere Golf Club was up.

They went looking for a flat in town. They found one in Newmarket and moved straight in.

I'd made the senior pennant team at the club, so I had new goals for my golf and new people to play with. I would remain a member there for the next decade and make some wonderful friends, some of whom are still friends today.

I visited Barry and Robin at the flat two or three times a week. Bryce had taught me how to play the guitar. Barry had shown me a thing or two as well, including 'Bad Blue', the song he had written and recorded. I remember playing Barry and Robin my full repertoire on the guitar. That's about three songs. While they were tucked up in bed, I'd serenade them, then head home.

It was late on a Sunday afternoon, on one of my visits, when Barry asked me what was open for a drink and a meal. I suggested we head out to one of the hotels by the airport. Barry put on his brown vinyl jacket, patted his thinning hair forward and the pair of us headed out. We found a hotel that looked busy enough and went inside.

A busload of tourists had just arrived and, for whatever reason, Barry decided to greet them all individually as they stepped down off the bus; he was very funny with his usual helping of charm. He won everyone over immediately, including the staff of the hotel, who couldn't believe Barry Crump was doing this with their guests.

After this impromptu meet and greet, Barry asked the staff if the restaurant was open. They said no, not for another hour or two, but the chef would make an exception for us and open the restaurant – just for our table for two.

We ate a great meal of steak, eggs, onion and chips. Barry

asked the waiter to run a bottle of red wine under the hot tap for a few minutes. We cleaned that up, too, as it washed down our dinner. No sooner had we demolished this, Barry said we'd like the same again - meal and wine. We were stuffed full.

We ended up with a small crowd at our table while Barry entertained us all. As you would expect, I paid the bill and we headed home.

I look back at my father at times like this and think what a gift he had.

But the signs were all there - I'd seen it before - Barry was getting ready to leave Auckland and the city life once again. He was accumulating funds with which to hit the road some time soon. He had recently done an advertisement for Scrumpy dog food. He'd also done some deal for which he was given a second-hand Vauxhall car as part of the payment.

We would still, every now and then, meet at Waitākere for a game of golf. Barry was driving me home after a game one day; I was in the back seat, with Barry and Robin in the front. When driving along Universal Drive in Henderson, Barry stopped and showed us a new ute on a revolving stand at the front of the local Toyota dealership. He said he'd really like one of those and told us to wait in the car while he went inside. As luck would have it, the manager had just come back from the annual Toyota conference in Wellington, where they were looking for someone to front their new range of utes coming out. Hollywood actors John Davidson and Robert Stack were international stars advertising for Toyota, but they were looking for someone local for the New Zealand and Australian market - then Barry walked in.

The relationship with his sidekick Lloyd 'Scotty' Scott and Toyota would last for the next fourteen years. The award-winning advertisements would launch Barry into living rooms around the country, bringing a whole new - and younger - audience to him.

Barry went on to receive a large salary and a new ute every year for the duration of their time together. None of this would happen for a few months - right now, there on Universal Drive, Barry and Robin needed running-around money.

I offered to buy the Vauxhall car they had just acquired, which I liked the look of, as I was selling my station wagon. I thought this might help the both of us. I did end up selling my car. I told Barry I'd be around to his place on Sunday to do a deal with him on the Vauxhall, if he wanted to. He didn't seem too keen on the phone, but I thought it didn't matter too much if he didn't want to sell it to me. When I turned up to the flat on Sunday, it was completely cleared out. Not a stick of furniture left, nothing. He'd gone.

I didn't understand. We had pretty much spent the best part of the year together, then this. Was it the car? Did he need more money for it? But he didn't know what I was offering. Nothing was making sense. Growing up, Mum had protected me from him and just this sort of thing happening, but she couldn't protect me from this - no one could.

Why couldn't he have simply said goodbye? I was in shock; I was hurt and confused. I don't know how long I stood there for before I went home.

A couple of months had gone past when the first of the Toyota ads came out on TV. Barry and Scotty were a huge hit. I noticed they used Barry's dog Bloke in one of the ads. That's the one where they went over a huge bump and had to wait for Bloke to land on the back of the ute. The ads were great - they were funny and they were clever. They sold a lot of Toyotas.

Six months after Barry and Robin had vanished, I was in Newmarket, picking up some items. As I was heading back to my car to head home, I walked straight into Robin.

Barry in Ōpōtiki, circa 1990 – with his trusty horse (which didn't, in fact, have antlers) and Bloke the dog.

'Martin!' she said, with a big smile on her face.

It was lovely to see her again. I knew leaving like that had not been her doing. We hugged with genuine affection.

Robin is not a tall person and, as I was hugging her, over her shoulder I spotted someone a few shop doors away, hiding. It was Barry. When he knew I had spotted him, he came out into the open with a very stupid 'okay, I've been caught' look on his face.

Robin said quickly, into my ear, how unhappy she was with how things had been left but couldn't talk Barry out of it. I wondered what his excuse could possibly be.

He said hi, mumbled something about the way they had left, and, as quickly as he could, left again. *Now my father is hiding from me, why? What did I do?*

I wanted to slap his head, hard. Now I *did* feel anger. Now I saw the gutless side of my father. He was hiding from his own son, who just wanted to love him, to know him. It took some time for me to calm down, but it would take years before I would understand why he did this - not just to me either, to all six of the sons he abandoned.

The years go on, like life does. I was out of the family catering business and had two catering contracts of my own - the Pukekohe Cosmopolitan Club and the Franklin Gentlemen's Club - which I was driving to each day: West Auckland to Pukekohe, four days a week.

I had help from friends running the Pukekohe club while I set up the Franklin club on my own. Then Bryce rolled into town. He needed money, a job, and somewhere to stay. I gave Bryce all he needed; he joined me at the Franklin club. He would often play the guitar in quiet moments, which everyone enjoyed as the guests started arriving in the restaurant.

He'd been with me no more than a few weeks when Barry

turned up one night, just after we'd opened the restaurant for service.

Bryce and I were flat out cooking for an early burst of customers, so we gave the meals to Barry to deliver to their tables. It was priceless to see the look on people's faces. At first, they weren't sure if it was actually him waiting their table. He didn't look too flash - he was dressed rough, but that was him and it made for great effect. You could hear the buzz going around the restaurant. Bryce and I thought this was so funny.

Barry stayed for a couple of hours, then disappeared into the night again.

I took a trip to Europe for nearly a year, during 1986–87. Then I came back to New Zealand to start up a new business, this time with Adele, my new partner. Before we could begin our working venture, we had to wait a few weeks. It was decided we would go for a South Island trip in my van. We threw a mattress in the back and left Auckland.

As part of that trip, we had arranged to meet up with Barry at a relative's place in Putāruru. It was the middle of the afternoon when Barry arrived, drunk. He was in the passenger seat, with Coonch, a boy of eleven or twelve who had just driven the pair of them all the way from Ōpōtiki. I couldn't believe it. None of us could. It's a nearly three-hour drive.

Barry got out, staggering.

'It's harder on me than it is on him. I worry all the way,' he said.

I've already mentioned Barry's fear of being caught drunk-driving. He was even prepared to risk the life of this young man to avoid it.

We stayed the night in Putāruru, where we all slept in the lounge. I watched Barry sleep, his chest rising between coughing and wheezing horribly from all his smoking and drinking. He looked uncomfortable. He sounded terrible.

In the morning, Barry drank whisky. We drank tea. I didn't think he was happy at all.

We hit the road. Adele and I followed Barry and Coonch. Yes, Coonch was still driving! We followed them all the way to Ōpōtiki.

Coonch drove beautifully, not one mistake or mishap. He stopped only once, on the long back road leading to Barry's property. We all got out to stretch our legs and have a chat. It was friendly as Barry and I shared a joint, and we all had a laugh as I put my arm around Barry's shoulder. I called him Dad for a joke, and he called me a cheeky young whippersnapper. I'm pleased Adele got a good photo of us in that moment.

As we were hanging about, Coonch walked around to the back of the ute and told the dog Bloke to get up. The dog, on cue, leapt out of the truck and ran straight up a bank next to the road, where we heard snarling and growling deep in the ferns. Then, with a very pleased look on his face, Bloke reappeared with a big possum in his mouth. He jumped back onto the ute and off we went again. That was the dog's dinner sorted.

Adele and I were both feeling a bit stunned, even disbelieving about this young man Coonch and what he was capable of.

You could only drive right up to Barry's house in the ute if the river was low. Otherwise, all mere mortals like ourselves used the swing bridge. It was an old farmhouse on quite a few acres, a property Barry and Robin had bought. I'm sorry to say that at this point they were no longer together.

We met Eileen, who they called Barry's housekeeper. She was actually his lover and the mother of Coonch, plus I believe seven or eight other children. Eileen was lovely. We got on great.

She and Barry drank a lot together; they told me they also

fought a lot, physically too, though I reckon Eileen wouldn't put up with too much of Barry's crap.

Eileen cooked on an old coal-range in the kitchen. There was something very comforting about the smell of the wood and the taste of Eileen's incredible roast dinner. She was good.

We stayed for four days. Eileen cooked for us the whole time and, never leaving the property, she made what food was there taste different and brilliant with each and every meal.

'It was friendly as Barry and I shared a joint, and we all had a laugh as I put my arm around Barry's shoulder. I called him Dad for a joke, and he called me a cheeky young whippersnapper.'

Barry's house was on the southern side of the property and didn't get a lot of sun. The clouds never lifted or left the place while we were there. At night, Barry and I played some guitar and he helped me with my rendition of the legendary 'Ballad of Eskimo Nell'. It's good to know how to recite it, but it's not mine

Barry and Martin share a joint
– and a laugh.

- I just borrow it every now and then.

There was a beautiful river on Barry's place, too. I was just throwing a stick for Barry's dog Bloke to chase when Barry snapped at me; he looked as if he was in physical pain. I'm now sure he was.

I ought to mention that Coonch was the inspiration for the young Māori chap, Ricky, in Barry's book *Wild Pork and Watercress*. Watching Barry and Coonch, they were so great together - as Uncle Hec and Ricky are in Barry's wonderful story. It was a pleasure to meet Coonch and spend time with him.

It was time for Adele and me to leave. Barry very kindly gave us a gas cooker for our journey south and we hit the road. The look on Barry's face made me think he'd like to be doing that.

A couple of years later, Adele and I got married. We sent Barry an invitation but never heard back.

LYALL I'd turned my back on the education system, my family and society in general. I had in some way killed myself, or the idea of who I was supposed to be.

I became a dole-bludging surfer, verging on unemployable. I grovelled and got hungry and just surfed. Piha was the perfect place for me, as there was always a wave. Winter was tough, though. Quiet, cold and lonely.

I wrote Barry a letter. I wanted some money. I seemed to be the biggest loser. 'Lie low, Lilo' was the taunt from the older crew.

I sat there in the dark on the steps of the closed general store. I had been going to ask for credit if they were open. A bacon and egg pie. I held the letter in my hand, thinking of the words I'd used. Writing to a writer. My handwriting was horrible and I was pleading for money, or maybe a car, I think. I stood up and had put the envelope in the post box when a girl burst out of the dark. It was the campground owner's daughter. I liked her.

I saw her at a party a few weeks later. She and I went outside, down the track to 'shady lane', and lost our virginity together. It felt like a sticky mess in the dark. She went home and I went back to the party. People were looking at me. Another girl asked me if I'd cut myself. Shocked, I went to the bathroom and saw I was covered in blood. I was the laughing stock around town for weeks.

My letter came back - return to sender. I packed a sack with clothes, a tent, my wetsuit, my surfboard and hitched out of town. I was going to see Barry.

I headed to Raglan, tenting at Manu Bay - surfing, eating, hitching, until I got lazy and kept my tent up all day. A chap from the council asked me to move along, so I headed over to the East Coast - surfing, making friends to never see again, feeling the love of community, and tenting wherever the day left me. I got well along the way toward Whangamatā. After a few weeks, I arrived in Ōpōtiki and, as luck would have it, Barry was home and I got a ride to his little hideaway from a bloke who knew him.

Being with Barry, his wife Robin and the dogs in the little hut I'd been in a few years previously was like wearing a warm coat in the cold of winter. The love I yearned for was little more than a faint shadow, but I clung to its warmth.

'So, what are you after, mate?' asked his missus when he was out of earshot.

'I just want to love him. That's all.'

After all the time on the road and waves under my feet, I'd forgotten that I was after nothing other than love. They suggested I take a few days to go around the East Cape.

I hitchhiked away and surfed at a bay till dark, then pitched my tent by the pub. When I got back a week later, Barry's wife told me he went looking for me and spent the night at the same pub I had my tent next to. It sounded like bullshit.

I stayed with them for a few more days then Barry gave me a speech, something about getting my own money and having to make my own way in life. It was then that I figured the letter I wrote might have found their eyes after all. They fed me on love and venison, and I was off again, back on the road to Māhia and Gisborne, once again feeding on the generosity of strangers.

A wee while after that, I arrived back in downtown Auckland at dark and hitched to Glen Eden, where my brother Al was staying. He was so happy to see me. He told me he thought I had gone away forever.

I was ready for a relationship. My heart had been broken and betrayed by a beautiful woman, after I did the same to another. I found more joy and freedom with a mountain bike - a purple Peugeot I pushed for an eternity, from National Park to Te Kuiti. That was my freedom and it gave me time to think.

But I chose to fall in love with her. A girl from the North Shore - dark hair, vivacious, an innocent bundle of love I wasn't ready for.

I took her to see Barry. The last time I'd seen him was four years earlier, when I was on my outdoors course coming back from the Motu. As usual, I had to hunt him down. He was living in a studio in Auckland, a space in a warehouse where he had all his books. He drank Elephant beer and smoked rollies, so I did too. He smacked her on her bum, which she seemed to enjoy. She ended up falling in love with him, visiting him in Wānaka when we had broken up. They seemed to love each other. Barry loved any cuddly woman, though.

I visited him a few times at the warehouse. He gave me his time and sometimes cash.

'Here, go get yourself a packet of smokes. You can stop smoking mine.'

I only smoked because he did; otherwise, I thought it was a disgusting habit.

'You've never met my parents, have you? Right, that's it - I'm taking you over to see them,' he said one afternoon.

A couple more beers and he announced he'd had too much to drink and couldn't drive. I offered to, but he muttered something indecipherable and became annoyed. It was time for me to shrink away. I could always tell when he'd had enough of my company. He became fidgety and quiet, like a storm brewing.

Barry gave me a shirt before rejecting me. I wanted to spend Christmas with him. I think he was just annoyed I had his phone number.

'Nah, mate. Sorry. I've got these Hare Krishna people coming over. It wouldn't be good to have you there.'

I got it. Loud and clear. He didn't want me around and he was putting up a façade to keep me at bay and keep charming my girlfriend. I didn't bug him again. I left him with the young Māori boy he'd taken under his wing. He let slip that he was annoyed with him for shooting slugs from the air rifle into his precious stack of books.

He'd always give me his latest book, which I would then promptly give away to someone else. I didn't want his books - I wanted his love. And a car, I wanted him to buy me a car. I was dreaming.

Another time, later on, I visited Mum and Dad and we talked about nothing much, but there was a forgiving warmth between us. I rode to the top of the hill on my new bike, the Tuatara. I knew every detail of that road and hardly needed my brakes. It was pitch black but I could sense and anticipate every bump and corner. A lady was walking up the middle of the road and I sensed her before I could see her and missed her by inches. I said a cheerful 'Hi!' as I zipped past her, giving her an unexpected fright.

I rode and pushed the Tuatara into the night and up the valleys, up Garden Road, into the scary dark bush, where I rested in silence. I slalomed the white lines up North Piha to the caves and ventured to the strongest spiritual place I knew of and asked for an answer.

'I didn't want his books – I wanted his love. And a car, I wanted him to buy me a car. I was dreaming.'

I rode again, stopped at the phone booth and gave Barry a collect call. He was living down south at this time. Before I did, I had to calm my breathing. I had been pumping the pedals for hours. Thoughts came and went, of memories and realisations. I knew I wasn't supposed to die and that I was here for a reason, but I didn't need to know what that was.

'Yeah, g'day, Lyall . . . everything all right?' he asked.

I could tell he thought I just wanted something. I told him my girlfriend had passed away, the one with leukaemia. I knew he had loved her. I also told him how I'd almost killed a few kids and a teacher. He went quiet then, likely because he'd been responsible for the death of several young men once, and was even charged with manslaughter for it. I told him about all the times I nearly died and tried to tell him how I was feeling, that I was invincible.

I can't remember what he said exactly but he invited me to see him and his latest wife, Maggie, down in Havelock. I hung up the phone, happy I'd made peace with both my fathers and, more importantly, with myself.

I rode around Piha, up the 'shady lane' shortcut along Rayner Road, up to Te Ahuahu Road, to the lighthouse and back to Pendrell Road, where I had to climb in the window. It was 3am by the time I turned in.

Another memory. My mate's birthday and his shout after a great day's skiing and snowboarding. He brought home whisky and beer that flowed through us like water. I was as drunk as I'd ever been and felt like smashing something. I started on an old piano, then got stuck into the old building out the back.

It wasn't the first time I'd lost control while drunk but this time it was different. This time, people got hurt. I had got myself into a rage and I didn't know why.

I kicked open the door and my mate and fiancée were hiding in the bedroom. I started in on her, throwing daggers of hate and fury. He got in the way, and as swift as the wind I had him with one hand around his throat, hoisting him off the ground, the other hand clenched at the end of an angry arm about to swing. His back was arched over the mantel above the fire and he was choking. He managed to splutter some words.

'It's my friggin' birthday, bro . . .'

I snapped out of it. I woke up to notice my lovely fiancée crying, pleading with me to let him down. He was going blue. I let him go and ran outside, hitting my head hard against the white power box. I saw the smashed piano and shed, and lay down in the grass. I knew I still had issues and realised I had to go and see Barry. I needed some answers.

If I were a cloud, I'd call trees my friends and play in
their tops
I'd glide up gullies and crests with ease, float up high,
cruise over seas
Something, though, would bring me back home to
Aotearoa
Where I could rest my head on a mountain and dangle
my feet in the ocean

I drove my fiancée's car full of our stuff to Havelock, where we dropped in on Barry and his wife.

They were pleased to see us, and I exuded a happy, contented energy. I wanted to let him know that I loved him and his new wife and her son who lived with them.

'Bag, make me a cuppa, would you? Bag, where are you? Bag . . .' Barry kept saying.

'Why do you call him Bag?' I asked.

'Baggage. He's baggage, that's why. I can't wait till he moves out.'

The boy must have been eight or nine years old. I thought it was all a bit mean but that was just Barry's way. Everything was a big joke. Things and people slotted into his way of speaking and doing things to follow his dream.

Barry and his wife had to go away for a couple of days so we stayed at his place in Havelock and looked after Bag. We were left a massive flounder we didn't know how to cook.

Barry being away gave me a chance to snoop through his things, his life I didn't really know. It was just as I imagined. He seemed stuck in yesteryear, in the 1950s or something, where everything had the musty smell of a tobacconist. Old books, writings and pens, guns, his wife's things. Condensed milk and salt, possum traps and tanning boards.

He hadn't allowed time, or anyone, to change him a bit.

'I thought it was all a bit mean but that was just Barry's way. Everything was a big joke.'

My fiancée and I enjoyed a season picking fruit at Motueka. A different orchard than we had been at before, with different people. We rented at the campground where a Māori couple were living in a bus. He was supposed to be a prophet. I was on a spiritual quest, so we visited with questions and connected that way. I can't remember what he told my fiancée but he told me I'd do well to attend an anger-management course.

I enjoyed riding the hills of Tākaka and exploring Harwoods Hole. I almost died as I pushed myself and the Tuatara through cliffs on the upper slopes.

We visited Barry's brother Bill and his zany German wife at Golden Bay. He told us about his spiritually gifted mother and violent, scary father. Time wore on and he became fidgety. I recognised the signs and we departed, tenting at Te Waikoropupū Springs.

Just as the picking season was ending, I had a vivid dream in which I threw my fiancée away like a piece of rubbish. I dismissed it, as we were excited to stay with Barry and Bag and Bag's mum.

We visited Barry and his wife again, bringing them a big bag of lovely pears that I joked they could throw at each other if they didn't like them. An awkward silence followed - I guessed they weren't always as blissful and fun as they made out. They seemed to drink a lot of booze and I was alarmed at how much salt Barry put on his food. He was fifty-nine but looked ninety.

'How much did you pay for that?' drawled Barry when I proudly showed off my fiancée's engagement ring.

'We got it in Taupō. Six-fifty,' I said.

He snorted. 'Six-fifty! Think of all the neat stuff you could get with that. Bloody waste!'

His wife shifted uneasily. They seemed very well off. Barry had bought her other sons flash Toyotas, which they apparently thrashed and got into trouble with. He spoke fondly of her sons, as though they were his own.

He wanted me to stay in some French bloke's house up the Sound so I could write a book. I was happy exploring the massive hills around Havelock and thrashing out poems I could hurt people's ears with. Barry hated my poems and it made me cry. His wife comforted me. Barry saw this and accused me of having a passionate embrace with his wife - I couldn't tell if he was joking.

We had been there a week or so and it was Barry's sixtieth birthday. They were having a party with his special friends, so my fiancée and I got the message and took off to Kaikōura. I surfed the famous waves and we gorged on crayfish. I had a thought of bringing the old man a big fat cray but didn't. I can't remember him ever getting me a pressie; I'm not sure he even remembered what month I was born. We got the vibe when we came back. I should have brought him one after all. Instead, I bought Bag a model aeroplane that we made and flew together.

My fiancée and I cornered Barry one day, when he was showing us his flash boat. We tried asking him some deep questions. He called me shallow and hollow like a log. He used the power of his vocabulary so I felt dumb and him smart. He put himself across like some type of spiritualist and told me that he didn't need to get to know me. I didn't need to get to know him, because I was him.

I had a set of unruly dreadlocks but I agreed to shave them off. Now I was a skinhead. The next day, Bag, Barry and I went for a proper adventure in the boat. Barry had taken us for a few token journeys in the shelter of the bay before but this time it was different. Just the guys this time, and we ventured right out to the mouth of Pelorus Sound, where we fished for tasty blue cod. The weather was perfect - blue sky on blue water, hardly a breath of wind. A perfect autumn day with my old dad and his boy.

'I want you to be a brother to Bag,' Barry said out of the blue. 'Even when I'm gone, I want you to be a brother to him. Promise me that, Lyall.'

I thought that was a bit cheeky but agreed and talked about Al and the younger brother I already had. My proper brothers. Then I asked him about Martin and Ivan and any other brothers or sisters I didn't know about. He got the point and declared the fish weren't biting.

We pulled anchor and he let me drive the boat into a little bay where he had a friend. It was about 11am and he cracked the top off a big bottle of Johnny Walker Red Label. The bottle would be empty by the time we headed for home.

His friend had a lodge that was idyllic, nestled into the bush. He disappeared and came back with fresh dope he dried on the stove. He did this three times before Barry insisted it was time to go.

The day was peaceful, fun and beautiful, one of those days that are hard to forget.

Clouds had gathered and a wind came up, making us late for the incoming tide. A vicious chop had developed and there was now a sense of urgency as we passed the mussel farms on the way to the shelter of Havelock. We just made it before dark and I reversed the trailer down with Barry's flash new ute. We rigged the boat onto the trailer and headed back to an empty home. I cooked a nice dinner of mashed spud, sausages and silver beet while Barry tracked the ladies down by calling around. He found them at the pub.

'Get home now!' he roared down the phone.

Lights came down the driveway as I was dishing up the dinner. I had it hot and laid out on plates.

I kissed my fiancée, who told me they'd been at the pub all day. Barry's wife reappeared in a silky dressing gown. Barry was playing his favourite music on the big stereo system - Dire Straits. He must have said something to work his wife up because she lost the plot and didn't care or notice that her dressing gown had come undone, exposing her nakedness.

After hurling her hate-spiked words, she grabbed a glass with a drunken hand and threw it at me, Barry and Bag. She grabbed another while the first one was still airborne. I sheltered Bag and my eyes. Barry just stood like a statue. The stereo got hit with a flying ashtray, the food was ruined, a beautiful statuette smashed the big television screen, there were cracked glass fragments in Bag's hair.

I knew I had to stay calm, even though I wanted to hold her and calm her down. She noticed me looking at her naked body and quickly covered up, in a moment of awareness. Barry took his opportunity and punched her between the eyes. She dropped.

There was a commotion outside and Barry motioned for me

to go and see what was happening as he dealt with Bag and his wailing mum. There had been complaints of violence and noise at the place before. Barry had a reputation to uphold; he had book sales from an adoring public in jeopardy.

I raced outside to see my fiancée kicking the door panels of the car her father had given her. She saw me and jumped into the driver's seat. I was too quick, intervening before she could lock the doors. She started the car and revved the engine. The last thing I wanted was for her to drive, as she was obviously extremely drunk. I was wrestling the keys from her and trying to get her to see reason.

Barry appeared, as silent as a deerstalker, and ripped open the driver's-side door. He pulled her out of the car by her hair and gave her a king-sized slap to the side of her head, flinging her like a ragdoll. He caught her with a slap to the other side of her head and she ran.

I was faced with a choice. Do I take on this beast of a man or do I run after my fiancée?

'Get after her!' he bellowed.

He didn't seem old anymore, and instead looked big and strong. I ran after my fiancée. A skinhead running after a woman on the main road of Havelock.

I grabbed her and we fought our way back into the drive. She had ripped my new jeans almost right off my legs. She had the strength of a mad woman and I was sitting on her when the police pulled down the drive, lights flashing but no siren. I was slammed onto the bonnet and arrested before being bundled into the back seat.

I could hear my fiancée talking with the cop. She had almost instantly calmed down and seemed sober, convincing him it was all just the booze talking. I was released from the cuffs and let out of the back of the cop car. It felt as though I had just swum the big rapid on the Motu after fighting to stay alive - it was the same feeling. I spoke with my fiancée, then she left with the cop.

I went back inside to the broken night, where an attempt had been made to clean up. The dinner I cooked went in the compost bin. I went to check on Bag, who seemed okay. As I walked back into the lounge, I silently thanked Mum for getting away from this scary man, my father.

Barry and his wife were laughing again, sipping out of a new bottle of whisky. I joined them and rolled a ciggy, trying not to look at her swelling, blackening eyes.

The next day, I took my fiancée's beaten car and picked her up. I felt like leaving her and remembered the dream I had had of discarding her like rubbish.

Back at the house, she tried being nice but Barry saw her and fired a cannon.

'Are you still here? Why don't you piss off, you boring bitch!'

She said goodbye to Bag and his mum.

'You want me to go, too?' I asked.

'No, you can stay. She has to go.'

I said goodbye to my fiancée and felt nothing but an empty void where my heart once sat.

Later on that day, we went to a vineyard for lunch. I wore a hat to hide my skinhead; Barry's wife wore dark glasses to hide her two black eyes.

Over the next few days, we drank and smoked and entertained Barry's friends and no one mentioned her black eyes and the glued-up treasures.

Bag, Barry and I adventured around Havelock, also visiting the pub where Barry pumped up his hero status among the old and alcoholic. I convinced him to take us to the trig station on the biggest hill on the other side of town. He drove like he did in the commercials and our bond grew.

In the back of my mind was my fiancée. I rung her place at Pukekohe. I got her father.

'It's for you, dear. It's that arsehole - what is he bloody after?' He made sure I could hear.

We had an awkward conversation with words that hid other words. We still had feelings for each other; it was the start of the end, filled with lust and hurt.

'Barry noticed and gave me a good serve. He saw himself in me, I reckon – irresponsible, irreverent, uncaring and not sorry.'

One drunken night, I gave Bag some of my beer and he got drunk. Barry noticed and gave me a good serve. He saw himself in me, I reckon - irresponsible, irreverent, uncaring and not sorry.

The next day, Al rang, very concerned about me. He knew the true nature of Barry more than I did, and cared for me more than Barry did. Barry was thrilled, as he loved Al, or Pogul, as he liked to call him.

Barry and I drove up to Picton the next day and met Al off the ferry. Al and I almost pulled an all-nighter, as memories and feelings flowed back into our minds.

Al wanted to get going back to his real life with his lady.

I didn't have a life to go back to but could tell Barry had had enough of me. Hints kept being dropped that I should've brought him back a cray from Kaikōura.

Al must have had a word to Barry because he announced that we were off to Blenheim to buy me a car. I was thrilled. The idea of hitching with my bike and surfboard wasn't fun. We visited a few car yards. I wanted the grunty muscle car but we settled on the cheap but solid Hillman Hunter. It was white and old and cost $700. My first car, finally.

We backed out of the driveway under a cloud of grim memories. Barry looked haggard and worn, and I felt bad as he waved a sad, tired hand that was trying to revamp an aging writing career. We made a drunken, wobbly drive through the night back to Al's place in Raurimu. I felt squeamish around his lady, my fiancée's sister. I felt like a failure.

On the set of a Toyota ad, early 1990s.

6.

Have I Got a Story For You . . .

He always did

‘I didn’t want to walk the few yards to my car to get more clothes as it would interrupt the story Barry was telling. I was under his spell – he had me.’

IVAN There was just one time that Barry expressed the desire to see me. I gave him a call and said I'd come around if he helped me write out the words to 'The Ballad of Eskimo Nell'. He agreed, so I met him in Henderson, where he performed a rousing rendition of the infamous ballad for me. It's infamous for more than one reason: one is that it's bawdy beyond belief, another is that there is no definitive version of it - there are several. Here's the version Barry and I wrote down together:

A few of the boys were whooping it up
In one of the Yukon halls
The guy in charge of the music box
Was steadily scratching his balls

The Faro kid had his hand on the twat
Of the lady that's known as Lou
And there on the floor on top of a whore
Was dangerous Dan McGrew

When out of the night
Which was black as a bitch
And into that din of a hole
Came in a dirty old prick

Fresh from the crick
With a rusty charge on his pole

As he shouldered his way
Through the flea-bitten crowd
He scratched the crutch of his pants
He looked like a man
With a dose of the clap
In the first stage of St Vitus' dance

His trousers were split
And covered in shit
As he squatted down on a keg
And his balls hung low
And he swung to and fro
Each time he moved his leg

'Don't look at me that way,
Stranger,' he said
I ain't shit
It's just this doggone syphilis
That's getting me bit by bit

My foreskin's all decaying
And my balls are red with rust
Each time I cough
A bit falls off
And mingles with the dust

When a man grows old
And his balls grow cold
And the tip of his prick turns blue

When it's bent in the middle
Like a one-string fiddle
He can tell you a yarn or two

So find you a seat
And buy me a drink
And a tale to you I'll tell
Of Dead-eye Dick
And Mexico Pete
And a girl called Eskimo Nell . . .

That's not even a quarter of the full ballad but, dear reader, it's likely best we leave it there - to call it eye-watering is an understatement. I guess there's a reason why it's so rarely written down. Suffice to say that Barry, usually in a smoky pub somewhere, with his iconic baritone voice, could somehow render 'The Ballad of Eskimo Nell' in such a way that it never seemed rude, even in mixed company.

MARTIN While I was hanging out with Barry playing golf in West Auckland, around 1980, my brother Ivan had settled in the Far North. He'd bought 140 acres in the Hokianga, on a river - a beautiful and remote property.

He'd gone and fallen in love with a local girl named Mary, who lived in a half-round barn with her family. Their property also had a beautiful river running through it. I think they must have bypassed the whole engagement part and went straight to the wedding, which we promptly received our invitations to attend. To my surprise, Barry said he was going.

It was a winter wedding, which was no trouble as the weather was good. I packed up my station wagon and threw a mattress

Ivan's wedding. Left to right: Barry, Mary, Tina, Ivan, Judith and Peter (Mary's parents).

in the back, so my accommodation was sorted. I headed north. Barry was also left on his own, in his VW van – Robin had their little hatchback car and I believe was using this time to catch up with her family.

Ivan and Mary were to be married in a gorgeous little church in the middle of a paddock on top of a hill, which you had to climb a fence to get to. It had corrugated iron over a couple of the windows. It seemed somehow fitting for a Crump wedding.

Family from both sides were there, with everyone talking, catching up and enjoying the occasion. I was talking to Mum when I noticed Barry and my stepfather Wally leaning on a fence jabbering away like long lost buddies. I was pleased Mum managed to get a photo of the two of them.

Ivan was getting a bit nervous, as Mary was over an hour late. When it got to an hour and a half late, I was serious when I told Ivan, 'Get in my car and we'll clear off. They can all get stuffed.'

It turns out Ivan got the time wrong. It was an 11am wedding, not 10am.

Mary, looking stunning in bare feet and with flowers in her hair, made her way across the paddock with her bridesmaids. They climbed the fence, and the ceremony began. It was lovely, and so was the reception back at Mary's family's property. We ate like kings – packhorse crayfish with other scrumptious delights.

As it was a morning wedding, by the early evening there were a few tired faces, and most were starting to head home.

Barry and I found our spot for the night in an abandoned quarry on Puha Road, not far from Ivan's place. We left the lights on our vehicles on until we built a fire and got it going. We brewed up some bush tea with condensed milk, got ourselves comfortable, sorted out our beds in our vehicles . . . then Barry started telling stories.

I was sitting on a log by the fire in shorts and a T-shirt. It was

Barry and Wally (Ivan and Martin's stepfather), Ivan's wedding.

getting late, and I was getting cold, but I didn't want to walk the few yards to my car to get more clothes as it would interrupt the story Barry was telling. I was under his spell - he had me.

While poking a stick into the embers, he asked, 'Did I ever tell you about the time when I was working for a furniture company with my mate Jim?' And he was off. Just like a child snuggling in for Sunday-morning radio sessions, I got myself comfortable to hear a yarn from the storyteller.

> It was a family business with about twenty staff all up. The owners were good people who looked after their staff and customers well - they also cared very much about their product, the furniture, which gave us all pride in our work and rubbed off on us.
>
> The owners were of Dutch descent and over half of the staff also had Dutch ancestry. All were decent folk except for one, Lars. He wasn't rotten through and through; there was just something about him that didn't sit right with everybody else. He always carried a big roll of cash on him that he flashed about whenever he could, to make himself look the big man. He was constantly looking to get the best of any deal from anyone, never caring too much about what was fair or right. Because of this, none of us would go out of our way to seek his company.
>
> So, when he asked Jim and I if we knew of any girls that would go out with him, we always said no, even if he did pull out the big roll of notes and say he'd pay for everything. Lars was so persistent, he

Martin's all ears as Barry spins another yarn.

just wouldn't give up, so in the end I caved in and told him I would set him up with a girl I knew.

I got in touch with Sue, a good sort. She had a bubbly personality and enjoyed a good time. I knew she was smart because she wouldn't go out with me. I told her about Lars and what we knew about him, but she was still willing to go out with him. She said that she was a big girl and could take care of herself. We told Lars on more than one occasion to treat Sue well and to do the right thing by her - which he promised he would do, flashing the bankroll at us again. This was Friday afternoon, so it wasn't until after the weekend that we found out just what happened between Lars and Sue.

It turns out he took her to a cheap Chinese restaurant for dinner - not a good start. He brought a cheap bottle of plonk with him, then it was back to Sue's place. He slept with her and stayed the night, but when he woke up in the morning she was gone. He jumped out of bed in a furious mood. He reached for his pants and noticed his roll of cash was not there. 'The bitch!' he screamed.

With that, he jumped up, squatted and shat right in the middle of Sue's bed, then wiped his arse on the curtains and pillowcases. He threw his pants on. Then as he reached for his jacket, he found his bankroll in the top pocket. Just then, Sue comes in the door with a very cheery 'Good morning', telling

> Lars that she bought the cigarettes he likes and has bacon and eggs for breakfast.
>
> Even Lars realised how low his behaviour is - he has no words, so he pushes past her and hotfoots it out of there, leaving his mess for Sue to clean up. He even had the cheek to carry on like all was normal on Monday morning at work.
>
> I'm pleased to tell you that Lars' big roll of notes went missing that week, and by some strange happening, it ended up at Sue's place.
>
> His behaviour with Sue also somehow reached the bosses of our company. They were not keen to have someone on their payroll who would do something like this, so, he was sacked.
>
> Things went downhill for Lars after that, I heard.
>
> And just so you know, Sue still won't go out with me. Smart girl, that.

It'd been some time since we last ate. I was starving. All we had to eat was pumpkin. I didn't like pumpkin, but we chopped some pieces up and put them in the camp oven on the fire. I ate it and enjoyed it. I didn't want the night to end.

Sometime late in the night, sleep got us both. In the morning we had a cuppa, then hit the road back to Auckland. Straight back into our routine. The following Monday morning, I met Barry on the first tee after his radio show. We had played the round and sat down for tea and a sandwich when Barry handed me a school exercise book, which is what he usually wrote his books in. The title was *Puha Road*, the place where Barry and I had just spent the night in the quarry.

I was excited as he asked me to proofread what he'd written, the book's first chapter. I don't know where Barry got his ideas from, but the story drew me in from page one. He went on to knock the draft manuscript out in just six to eight weeks. I loved it - the characters, the journey, the twist at the end. This, in my humble opinion, is one of his true gems.

Sometimes, while playing golf on the hills of Waitākere, we would sit down and catch our breath. One frequent place was the fourteenth tee. It was set back into the bush, so we had shade. I was telling Barry a story of my own this particular day and, absent-mindedly, I said to him, 'You should have been there.' Then I carried on with my story.

It must have been weeks later when Barry came back to me.

'You know when you were talking to me a while back and you said I should have been there?'

I had to think for a bit but I did remember.

'Well, you were right. I should have been there.'

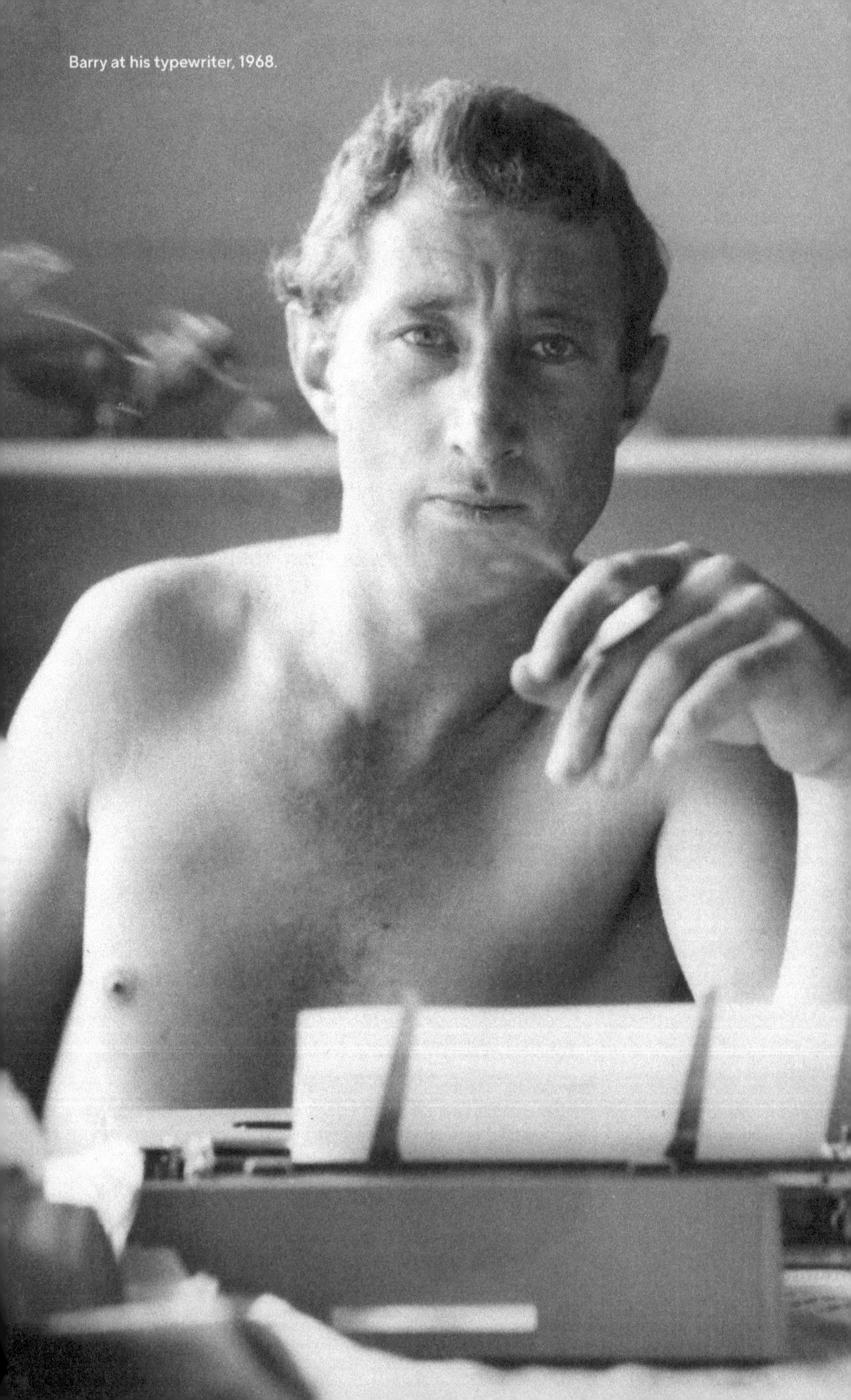
Barry at his typewriter, 1968.

7.

A Way With Words

The Barry most people knew

‘The press was raving about the great new storyteller – Barry Crump had arrived, with lethal charisma.’

MARTIN During the 1960s, Barry married twice. First to the well-known poet of the time, Fleur Adcock. She was a fragile type who liked the finer things in life. She thought the rough Kiwi bushman could be tamed. Barry? He cheated on her the night before their wedding.

He often got drunk and hit her. To finish off his whole dismal performance, he did an awful job as a stepfather to her son Andrew. The marriage lasted only five months - it was doomed before it started.

Fleur, now in her eighties and living in England, has been quite public about their marriage. She has said she and her son are still traumatised by the treatment they received from Barry. It's a shame they were both so affected by their time with Barry. Mum just hit the prick back.

When Barry met Fleur, he also met her group of friends, including author and poet Kevin Ireland, who was starting up a new magazine called *Mate*. Kevin thought that Barry should have a go at a short story for its launch.

Kevin suggested to Barry that, if he wanted to become an author, he should read. So Barry loaded up Kevin's personal collection of books in his car and did just that. He read them all: Charles Dickens, Banjo Paterson, Lewis Carroll, Mark Twain, Dylan Thomas and many more.

Barry with Fleur Adcock, 1964.

It was around this time that Barry also read a book on hunting by a Canadian author that he found deathly boring. He reckoned he could do better.

Barry would write twenty-four books during his life. Most took a relatively short time to complete, between four and eight weeks, but his first novel took considerably longer. He would later boast that he knocked it out in a month - the truth is it was more like two years.

Barry, with Mum's prompting, wrote a lot of *A Good Keen Man* at our place on Astley Avenue, but at the time he had a new girl, Jean Watson, who was also a writer. He felt free again. He had a new determination to finish his book, and he did.

A Good Keen Man was finally done. He headed off to find a publisher.

Barry was rejected several times, being told that such a story would never sell - Whitcombe & Tombs, one of the biggest New Zealand publishers of the time, would reject him outright. They said it would make no profit 'to you or ourselves' - a decision the company would later deeply regret.

Barry posted the manuscript to A.H. & A.W. Reed in Wellington and, as fortune would have it, it landed on the desk of one Ray Richards. Ray read Barry's book in its raw state. He understood the hunting life and he loved Barry's humour. He saw a future in it, but made Barry use his own name as the lead character - the only book of Barry's to ever do so. Reed gave him a £50 advance.

Barry then went bush with Jean - he'd had his fill of city life for the time being - while Reed got Barry's yarn into print.

Barry and Jean had been rabbiting for a couple of months when word reached them that all hell had broken loose on *A Good Keen Man*. Its success amazed everyone. It had to be reprinted time and time again. The demand was huge. The press was raving about the great new storyteller - Barry Crump had arrived, with lethal charisma. Well, it all helped with sales. The book would go on to be reprinted an astonishing fourteen times.

'Barry also read a book on hunting by a Canadian author that he found deathly boring. He reckoned he could do better.'

Barry now couldn't go to the pub without being recognised. He had money and fame - just what he was after. But he didn't handle either very well. Over the next five years, Barry wrote more books, with good to reasonable success. He took Jean to Australia, out in the Gulf of Carpentaria, where they hunted huge saltwater crocodiles. This adventure was turned into a great yarn and published as the book *Gulf*.

Soon after Barry arrived back in New Zealand from his Aussie adventure with Jean and the crocodiles, he was offered a role in an English movie being made here by director John O'Shea. The movie is called *Runaway*.

Barry played the small part of a reclusive bushman called Clarry. I watched it. It was awful.

Barry at Lizard Island, Great
Barrier Reef, Queensland.

Instead of using Barry's deep and gravelly voice, they gave him a high, shrill whine - it was just wrong.

Sure, he could now include actor on his list of accomplishments, but I wouldn't brag too much about it.

'Barry was asked to judge a beauty contest in Hawke's Bay. It was like inviting a fox into the chicken coop.'

When spending time with Barry, you never knew when you were going to be entertained by some story he'd roll out. He seemed to have an endless supply of them. There was the one, as they say, about the beauty contest . . .

Being well known did offer up opportunities in the mid-1960s, and Barry was asked to judge a beauty contest in Hawke's Bay. It was like inviting a fox into the chicken coop.

He arrived on the Friday and started drinking. He met all of the ten contestants. The contest ran on the Saturday and finished with the grand crowning on the Sunday.

Now, let's be honest, Barry was not just rough in nature - he was a bit rough to look at as well, with a face like a road map. But he was living proof of what charm and storytelling can do.

He reckoned that, by the Sunday night, he had slept with

nine of the ten contestants. He then told the last one what he had done and that he felt a bit sorry that she had been left out, like she was missing out on something wonderful.

Yes, you guessed it, according to him he drove back to Auckland with a perfect ten.

When telling me this yarn, it wasn't like Barry was boasting; more like simply relaying something that had happened. I'd love to know how this kind of thing *just happened* to him. I'm not sure how true it is, but I've never forgotten the story, and so his myth and legend grows.

In late 1968 Bryce Peterson challenged Barry to write a song himself, if he thought it was that easy. That's all the prod Barry needed, and, within a week, he had written the song 'Bad Blue', about a dog that gets up to a whole lot of mischief.

It was soon organised for Barry to meet a guy named Paul Harrop and his band on a Saturday morning outside the famous Stebbing Studios in Herne Bay. They met, went over the song once, then recorded it in one take.

The song wasn't terrible. Another string to the bow of the bushman.

IVAN To get a handle on Barry, you're probably best to read his books. His philosophy is explained in the characters: Barney the Dough Roaster, Quinn, Harry and, of course, Barry's own favourite, Sam Cash.

Though my brother Lyall most looks like Barry, I've been maybe a bit closer in lifestyle and proclivities. I was possibly even crazier: explosives, guns, drugs and fast machines.

The day Barry finalised
his divorce from Robin.

MARTIN If you ever get a chance, read Robin Lee-Robinson's book *In Salting the Gravy: a tale of a twelve year marriage to Barry Crump*. It's an incredibly honest read of just how frightening it could get being around Barry when he was at his darkest and worst.

'Barry was the public face for Toyota utes and they were selling well. In the early 1990s, Barry was receiving a new-model ute every year, plus a salary.'

In 1992, Barry wrote his own autobiography, which he called *The Life and Times of a Good Keen Man*. I remember Mum receiving a heap of calls from Barry for help, as his memory for dates and happenings was not too good. The book barely scratched the surface of his life.

If you want to read the best and fullest account of Barry's life, Colin Hogg's *A Life in Loose Strides* is it. It captures the bushman's life from start to finish so well and is superbly written.

Barry was the public face for Toyota utes and they were selling well. In the early 1990s, Barry was receiving a new-model ute

Barry recording a reading of *A Good Keen Man*, likely for radio broadcast.

every year, plus a salary; he'd never had such a regular income before. It's a shame so much of it was spent at the liquor store.

At one Toyota conference, there was a keynote speaker talking to the audience when they heard, all of a sudden, a chainsaw start up behind him. Someone was cutting a door out of the wall! Then it got booted down and out walked Barry Crump to tell everyone present how these Toyotas really work. It was a stunt, of course.

Meanwhile, Mum was not doing so well. She was unhappy. It bothered me enough that Adele and I moved back home for a while, so I could be near Mum.

Mum was always the strong one, the one who we would go to, but she was vulnerable at this time. Mum and Wally were not getting on. Mum wanted to leave. I talked to Wally about it. He was hurting bad, too. He'd had more than one affair and been caught, so he could hardly complain too much, but it still hurt.

Mum shocked us all by telling us she was going to join Barry on his upcoming Toyota promotional tour. She told me that she would stay with him . . . until he turned. I knew exactly what she meant. It was a compromise.

She left and went on tour with Barry. She was gone for several weeks. Mum got a change and some attention. When she arrived back home, Mum told me it went exactly as she had said it would. She stayed until he turned. So that was the end of that.

Mum looked and sounded much better. Whatever happened on tour stayed on tour, and we got Mum back.

ERIK It was never a secret who my real father was. I knew that he was some sort of author, though I knew little else about him.

Tina – while on tour
with Barry.

When I was around seventeen, the Toyota ads started appearing on TV. Mum said that that was Crumpy, my father. My heart seemed to beat more loudly as I stared, mesmerised, at the outrageous exploits of this swaggering character and his sidekick Scotty. It felt absurd. Could this man really be my dad?

'The Crumpy ads kept coming. They might be selling a car, but to me they were selling a father.'

As the years went on, the Crumpy ads kept coming. They might be selling a car, but to me they were selling a father. Every time, I would stop and watch, captivated. Even though our only connection was through a TV screen, that man was part of my life. Over time, the ads reignited the feeling of lack, and, perverse as it might sound, I began to miss the parent I never had.

Barry, Ōpōtiki, mid-1980s.

8.

The Long Goodbye

A father is gone

‘As I got older and the searing memories of my childhood faded, the feeling of something missing grew stronger.’

IVAN All my life, Barry's popularity has been a factor. There's hardly much chance to just be yourself when that pressure is so constant. Imagine what it was like for him. A good reason to avoid fame like the plague.

When I had a bit to do with him, in his later years, I couldn't help but notice that public life sucks. His reputation has influenced me a lot. There are thousands of people who told me they had drunk or hunted with him - that's if they had actually done it. The same phenomenon has happened by osmosis somehow to me. People seem to remember me, and some make up weird stories, which I swear aren't true.

MARTIN I saw Barry pop up every now and then, on TV or in the paper. It was good to see him be honoured with an MBE for his contribution to New Zealand literature in 1994. This is when he made the quip, when receiving his medal at Government House in Wellington, saying how good it would look pinned to his Swanndri.

They even put his face on a stamp. I saw him sing with Scotty when New Zealand won the America's Cup in 1995. He looked overweight and older than I'd seen him before - he'd aged a lot.

Adele and I had had our first child - my beautiful bundle

Barry and Lloyd 'Scotty' Scott, iconic faces of the Toyota ads for twelve years, through the 1980s–90s, here perform 'Sailing Away' as a part of the 1995 America's Cup celebrations.

Georgia. She was fifteen months old and in my arms when Barry rang me at home one day, much to my surprise. We hadn't spoken for a few years. He sounded good.

He told me that he had married his fifth wife, Maggie. He said he'd told her that she would like me, which was nice to hear. They'd bought a property together at Welcome Bay, Tauranga. He seemed to be enjoying life again. I talked to Maggie briefly. She sounded lovely. Barry heard Georgia in the background, and I told him that was his granddaughter. He liked that. He said we should visit them when we could. I agreed. It was a good call.

I didn't know at the time that it would be the last time I'd ever speak to my father.

It was six days later, on a Wednesday, just after lunch, when Barry's younger brother, my uncle Colin, rang me. He told me to come to Tauranga Hospital immediately - Barry was very sick and had had emergency surgery. Come now, he said.

I told him I'd get hold of Ivan and that we would come down together. Getting hold of Ivan was not easy - he lived way off-grid. His phone was inside an old ammunition case on top of a fence post by a cattle stop, on the boundary of his and the neighbour's property, with only cows in the surrounding paddocks to hear it ring. There was a red vinyl chair under the phone, so you had somewhere to sit down if you ended up there for a while. What was in my favour was that Ivan had fathered ten children and the odds were that someone would be passing by in the afternoon after school finished.

So I rang at three-thirty and, by some miracle, I got Ivan's wife, Mary, on the phone. I told her about Barry and that I would wait for Ivan to come down before I would leave. She then walked the rest of the way to the house and told Ivan, and he got to me as quick as he could. We arrived at Tauranga Hospital at around 10.30pm. Colin had gone back to Auckland. It was then

Left to right: Mary (Ivan's wife), Ivan
and Barry in the Hokianga, 1981.

that Ivan and I met Maggie for the first time.

After all the abuse he'd unleashed on his own body over the years, Barry had decided to get physical, to get back in better shape. Barry and Maggie had bought their house and a few acres, and it needed work. He had tackled the fencing first, heavy work for someone who'd not been doing a lot of anything physical.

He soon called out to Maggie to ring the physio, as he had put his back out. When they arrived at the physio's clinic, Barry said that it was his stomach that was now hurting, not his back. He then collapsed. They called an ambulance and he was taken straight to Tauranga Hospital.

It turns out it was neither his back nor stomach. He had an aneurysm in his main aorta and it had ruptured. His body had been filling up with blood. They operated on him for six and a half hours.

We met the doctor when we arrived, and he told us it was touch and go, and that we ought to watch the monitors around him overnight to see if there were any improvements. The doctor said he would see us in the morning and then left.

Maggie is a very nice person, and she was holding up okay. I watched her with Barry; she was rubbing his feet. There was no doubt that she loved him. It didn't look much like Barry, to be honest - this huge, swollen person in the bed with tubes everywhere.

We got to know Maggie a little better as we spent this time together, talking and watching the monitors through the night. At no time did we discuss, or even think, that he wouldn't pull through. I mean, he was Barry Crump - he was tough; in my mind, he was almost invincible. He couldn't die.

It was just after 6am when Ivan and I went for a walk to get a coffee. We agreed that it was not looking good - the monitors had shown that Barry's condition had got worse overnight, not better. It was starting to dawn on us that this could be the end.

When we got back to Barry's bedside, Maggie agreed with us that things were looking grim. This was when the doctor joined us. He said that they'd used instruments to look inside Barry and not one of his organs was in good enough shape to kick in and help. He said Barry's lungs were 'like glue'.

He asked us whether we were aware that Barry had been having heart trouble, as there was scarring on his heart going back years. The doctor told us he would have been in serious pain with it, but Barry had said nothing.

More than once, Barry had mentioned he was world-weary and ready for the next life. He might finally have got his wish.

We knew that Barry didn't like hospitals. It was at this moment that we all agreed his time was up. Barry was gone, but the doctor said he would give us two hours to say goodbye. He said that if he turned off the life support straight away, it could be unpleasant, with nerves jolting the body around, so he would gradually let Barry go.

We were stunned. How could this be?

It was close to 10am when we watched him take his last breath.

On 3 July 1996, at sixty-one years old, Barry Crump died.

We thanked the doctor and left.

It was amazing how quick word got around. We hadn't even left the car park when a helicopter was landing on the hospital grounds with reporters on board.

I drove Ivan back to Auckland. I nearly fell asleep on the way home – I really had to concentrate to stay awake. When I arrived home, I had over fifty messages waiting for me, three of them from the *Holmes* show. I lay down but couldn't sleep. I called and thanked those who had rung and left their condolences. I also spoke to the *Holmes* show – I was going on with Paul at 7pm.

I couldn't turn on a radio or TV without hearing the news.

Barry receiving his MBE in 1994, for services to literature – and famously quipping that the medals would look good pinned to his Swanndri.

It was everywhere. I was still without sleep when I appeared on the *Holmes* show that night. Barry's death took up the whole half-hour programme. I felt guilty afterwards; I had enjoyed my time with Paul on his show on the same day I'd lost my father. *What's wrong with me?* I thought.

I struggled to go to or even give a thought to work for the week between Barry's death and his funeral. I was very restless. The day of the funeral was a circus; so many people. TV even turned up to film the event. As Barry was a Bahá'í, and it was customary for them to be buried within ten kilometres of where they had died, the funeral was held in Tauranga. The actress Ilona Rogers, also a Bahá'í, led the ceremony.

A number of people, including myself, said a few words. Then it came time to take the casket to the grave site. What a procession.

Barry's coffin was lowered into the grave. I was standing there looking down on the coffin when I was joined by Tim Shadbolt, who had previously been our mayor in Waitākere (where he famously towed his concrete mixer with the mayoral Rolls Royce). He was now the mayor of Invercargill. Tim thought it was good time to tell a yarn - he was right, it was. I can't remember all of the story except that it was about Barry meeting Michael Hill, some time at some place. The yarn ended with Michael shaking Barry's hand and saying, 'Michael Hill, jeweller.' 'Barry Crump, wanker,' came the reply.

It was just right and so fitting to have a yarn told at the storyteller's gravesite - thanks, Tim.

I met and saw so many people that afternoon. One was the well-known photographer Ans Westra, who told me I had a brother I may not be aware of - her son Erik. I thank her for that.

It was also great to see Margo, Barry's girlfriend from some time back. She pulled me aside and said, 'You know, Martin, that when the tall tree falls, it lets the light in on the smaller trees so they can grow.' We hugged, and she smiled and left. What she said had an immediate impact on me.

That night, we all met in town at a favourite bar of Barry's, where we were served his favourite drink, Johnny Walker Black Label. There seemed to be an endless supply, and the party atmosphere lasted well into the night.

It must have been around midnight when I spotted Tim Shadbolt, who had his tie around his forehead and was telling all who listened that he was Barry Crump's love child. Tim, with a friend, had driven all the way from Invercargill to Tauranga in an old Chrysler with no heater, so they stopped and bought a gas heater, which they lit in the car! What an effort Tim had put in to be there. I'm very pleased he did.

ERIK As I got older and the searing memories of my childhood faded, the feeling of something missing grew stronger. I left home, started a career of my own writing computer software, and was a successful loner.

As the years passed, though, the urge to connect with my father grew, and I decided that one day I would go and meet him. But I was busy forging a life of my own, so I kept putting it off.

Then, one day when I was thirty-one, I wandered into a dairy to buy a pie. As I waited in line to pay, standing listening idly to the store's radio, the news came on:

NEWS JUST IN OF THE DEATH
OF A FAVOURITE KIWI CHARACTER.
NEW ZEALAND LOST A LOVEABLE LEGEND
TODAY: BARRY CRUMP HAS DIED AT 61,
AFTER A HEART ATTACK.

I froze, gazing at a spot on the floor. My ribs felt too big for my chest and icy worms seemed to slither across my back. *He's dead?*

THROUGH BOOKS, FILM, TV AND SONG,
AND EVEN A STAMP, HE WAS PART
OF EVERYDAY LIFE.

I stared around the store, barely able to breathe. People were standing behind me, looking bored, and I was almost at the counter. I didn't know what to do. This was my father, a part me. Should I scream, rant, cry? I felt like a shell inside of me had cracked, but all I could do was feign indifference.

BARRY CRUMP DIED AT TEN O'CLOCK
THIS MORNING AT TAURANGA HOSPITAL,
SURROUNDED BY FAMILY AND CLOSE
FRIENDS, AFTER LYING UNCONSCIOUS ON
A VENTILATOR FOR TWO DAYS.

I'd always told myself that I had no particular attachment to him, that I had been happy growing up as part of a single-parent family, and now I was happy to be alone, but the feelings still roiled up within me like a thousand angry ants. I had pretended that his absence hadn't mattered, but in quiet moments I would think of other people's families and what it must have been like to grow up with a father who loved you.

The guy behind me grunted. The till was free, so I buried the turmoil, paid for my pie and wandered quietly outside.

For days, the feelings swirled around, but I felt there was nothing I could do. I had honestly intended to go and visit him some day, to talk to and see who my father was, but now it was too late. I had lost my chance.

Looking back, that moment in the dairy had a huge effect on my psyche. While I was growing up in a single-parent family and with an abusive stepfather, I had often felt anger, sadness, even despair, and I had learned to wrap those feelings up inside my shell. Then, once my stepfather had gone from my life, I had tried to break free, to let my feelings out, but that moment in the dairy changed things again.

'I had honestly intended to go and visit him some day, to talk to and see who my father was, but now it was too late. I had lost my chance.'

Listening to the news of my father's death but being unable to react sealed up those emotions again. Surrounded by strangers in that crucial moment, I had felt my only choice was to not let it get to me - and so it didn't. I shut those feelings away and today they are all but gone.

Barry's funeral was on the following Monday. Mum asked if I wanted to attend. I considered it, but felt that bridges had already been burned - besides, it clashed with a compulsory on-campus course for an extramural paper I was doing. I'd fail the paper if I didn't attend, so I used that as an excuse not to go to the funeral.

HARRY In my early twenties, I went to a counsellor and he suggested I write a letter to my father. Not one you send, of course. In that letter, I said I would piss on his grave.

Many years later, long after I'd forgotten about the letter, Barry died. Uncle Colin said Barry had been drinking a 750ml bottle of whisky a day.

'The booze got him,' so reckoned Uncle Bill. I believe he was probably right.

Mum and I drove from Wellington to Tauranga for Barry's funeral. We thought we saw Lloyd Scott, the actor from the Toyota ads, overtake us on the way, but we didn't see him at the funeral.

Mostly I was furious that day. There were people who hardly knew Barry who talked for what seemed liked hours. Media poking cameras into family business. Uncle Colin told me to push in as a pall bearer, supplanting one of Barry's newly adopted teenage stepsons. Poor bugger almost fell off the stage. But when your uncle tells you to do something - you do it.

Uncle Colin was as clever as Barry. 'You might as well be sitting on it,' he said to Uncle Bill as we carried the coffin up some steep stairs.

At the gravesite, my knees went weak as I imagined pissing into my father's grave, even though my letter from years prior had been all but forgotten. My brothers picked me up by the elbows. I think they thought I was grief-stricken - but it was, I believe, a processing of fury. Nowadays, I think of my father as a brilliant man who wasn't given a decent chance.

STEPHEN I was in Australia when I heard the news that Barry had passed away. I remember feeling sad because of the finality of it. No chance now to see him again.

I felt it was a shame because of how young he was and I thought about what else he could have done if he had taken better care of himself. I tend not to analyse things too much - I usually just accept things as they are and move on - but I've thought about that a lot.

LYALL A year after I had last visited Barry, he died. I can't say I was surprised.

I met Harry at the funeral, and we and his other sons lowered Barry's heavy body into the earth. I made a little speech and ended up getting angry, calling him a bastard.

Everyone went back to a pub and I drank whisky with famous people and hardly an ill word was spoken. He was still a hero when talking over a bottle of whisky and a beer. Tobacco and dope smoke filled the air, and I passed out in the gutter in front of the pub. I could hear people concerned about me. Bag came out and cared for me until his mum took us home to their place in Welcome Bay. Her other sons were there and I remembered the promise I had made to Barry. I was Bag's brother - for the next day, anyway. It would have been weird for me to stay in touch.

As I was leaving, Maggie, Barry's widow, asked me what I wanted. There were his guns and possum traps for the taking. I grabbed a .22 and left for Auckland, leaving behind memories of a father I'd never really had.

MARTIN After Barry died, I was surprised to hear, out of the blue one day, from Maggie, his last wife, who kindly invited me to visit. She seemed a little nervous, but we got on well.

She very generously gave me Barry's medals, the OBE

and MBE he'd received for his contributions to New Zealand literature. I gratefully accepted them. It was right after this that I heard from Uncle Colin. He requested I visit him at my earliest convenience, so I did.

'I grabbed a .22 and left for Auckland, leaving behind memories of a father I'd never really had.'

He was not happy and had been having words with Maggie about Barry's will, which he handed to me. It read something like: 'I leave everything to my wife Maggie. I want no squabbling over my possessions.' That was it.

I didn't know what to think. Colin really had the bit between his teeth, saying to me, 'That woman has no right to anything and should hand it all over to us.'

Colin was still hurting, obviously, but I was thinking Maggie owned her own home, which she put into the relationship with Barry, so of course she had some entitlements. How could she not? I struggled to understand what was really upsetting Colin so much, as Maggie's contribution was clear to see.

Within two weeks, I'd been roped in to go on the *Holmes* show with Colin to talk about the feud going on between Maggie and the Crump children. There was no such thing, of course - Colin and Maggie, more like it. It was ugly.

Colin was angry; Paul Holmes was angry, too, for whatever

reason. He was screaming at his crew right before we went live to air. A bad start.

Colin was demanding that everything be handed back to Barry's abandoned children. No compromises, no discussion. That was his deal. Maggie was not even there to defend herself. I don't know if she was asked to appear - you would think so, but regardless, her not being there didn't seem right.

Paul asked me for my thoughts on this. I acknowledged the love I had witnessed from Maggie to Barry, and that she was, of course, entitled, but said there was just one thing that bothered me. Barry and Maggie were only together for two years and there was a large body of work completed over a lifetime, which I thought should come back to the Crump family. That is where the interview ended. It all felt rotten.

Within weeks, I was back sitting with Colin at his place. He had hired a well-respected and expensive law firm in the city to represent us against Maggie. It had come to that. He promised that he would pay for all the law firm's expenses and informed me that he was not allowed to challenge Maggie - he had tried, but the lawyers told him that only the children of Barry could legally contest the will.

Colin said that I had to lodge my intent with the lawyer by 7 December, which was only three months away. I was to do this or everything would go to Maggie forever.

I asked him for some time to consider it all. He handed me some paperwork to take with me and I left.

At this stage, I was thinking I wouldn't be contesting the will. I didn't need the hassle and, importantly, it just didn't feel like the right thing to do.

I talked to Adele, Mum and Wally about it. They didn't feel strongly about it either way but would back whatever decision I made. Ivan said that we shouldn't challenge it because, as

Barry himself stated in the will: 'I want no squabbling over my possessions.' Like Ivan, I tended to agree with this – it would be honouring Barry's wishes.

Time was pretty much up. I had to decide one way or the other but I was starting to have second thoughts. I'd been hearing about my brothers, even the ones I'd not yet met. Some of what I'd heard was a little disturbing. It had not been easy for them.

'He didn't acknowledge that I or any of my brothers ever existed. Is that what we meant to him? Nothing? We weren't worth even a mention?'

They'd had so little of anything from their father, other than being abandoned and hurt. I knew that Maggie's children were being put through King's College. Barry's stepchildren had been given expensive educations care of him, yet his own children didn't get so much as lunch money.

Then I read the will again – it was short, it was clear, but it was wrong. I ultimately decided to contest the will. I fought hard with myself over this decision. You see, I'm the nice guy, I don't make waves or ruffle feathers. I couldn't give a shit about his possessions – it's that he didn't acknowledge that I or any of my brothers ever existed. Is that what we meant to him? Nothing? We weren't worth even a mention?

If he had said, 'To my children Ivan, Martin, Stephen, Harry, Erik and Lyall, here's a pair of socks each, and I wish you well,' I would never have contested the will. But Barry got this wrong and I wasn't having it.

I lodged my intent with the lawyers on 6 December. Maggie got word from her lawyer about what I had done and invited me to visit her again. I went.

She knew that I wasn't doing this to her personally and suggested we cut out the lawyers and court costs and settle on a deal where I would assist her as the rights holder, and help generate funds through the Crump estate for a few years, then, when I took over the rights, she would come in with me for a few years. At that time, I didn't see the full value of this, so no deal was struck. I think now perhaps I should have accepted it. We all could have done without lawyers and the press. Maggie was rightfully fighting for herself and her children. I was fighting for what I thought was right.

The case was held in the High Court at Auckland with TV cameras and reporters about. That night on TV was all about this great feud between Maggie and me, fighting over Barry's carcass and whatever we could get our hands on. It was awful, and bloody untrue.

At the end of the court case, I, alone, was awarded the Crump copyright, in its entirety, to kick in on 12 October 2007 - nine years away. This date was given as it was when Maggie's youngest child was to graduate from King's College.

Maggie got the house and grounds. During the years following Barry's death, she received some pretty healthy royalties on book sales. Her children's education at King's College was paid for.

Maggie sold Barry's hat, gun and other personal possessions by auction for $27,000 to a property developer in Kerikeri. I didn't have the money to bid on any of these items, otherwise I would have, but the developer did a very cool thing and put it all on display in a museum in Kerikeri. I'm happy for all of this. I would have liked the copyright a bit sooner, but too bad - this was it.

Then I found out through the lawyers that Uncle Colin had pulled out of paying the legal bills! He had paid the first and only bill he was going to pay, I was told. He didn't even ask me to visit to share this news.

A few years earlier, Adele and I had bought Astley Avenue off Mum and Wally, who were now living up north. By the time the court case was over, Adele and I had to sell the house to pay the lawyer's bill. The house the family had owned since the mid-1950s, where me and my brothers had grown up, where my own children were born, where Mum and Barry were married, where all our childhood memories are, was gone.

A reporter for the *Herald on Sunday* wanted to do a piece on the fact that Colin stopped paying the bills as promised. I sort of knew him. I told him my side of the story and his headline that followed read, in capital letters: 'A GOOD KEEN PENSION PLAN'. I was disgusted.

With all the very public exposure on the case, I did cop a bit of flak from those I knew, and from strangers, about how rich I now was and that I wouldn't have to work again. I didn't say a thing but I wanted to yell at them all. The truth was I'd just lost my family home and I was in debt. What did I win?

I hold no anger towards Uncle Colin. I'm glad he told me all the things he did about the legal process but also events as they related to Barry's father and their family. The truth is, I would have contested the will even if he wasn't paying the bills. That, of course, would have put an enormous strain on Adele and me, and it turned out it did anyway.

Adele and I eventually broke up, not just over losing our home but more to do with my dreadful behaviour. You think I would have learned and known better. We divorced but remained good friends, I'm so pleased to say. We have both remarried.

I am now married to Jill, who I knew when we were young. It turns out we have children with the same names. Jill's daughters are Olivia and Georgia, and my daughters with Adele are Olivia and Georgia. They are also of a similar age.

Barry, late 1980s/early 1990s.

9.

Legacy

The shadow remains

‘They only wanted to show a brute, a violent one, which he certainly could be, but it wasn’t all that he was.’

MARTIN The twelve months following Barry's death were a restless time for me. I was losing interest in my work, and I kept thinking about what Margo had said to me at the funeral.

I was invited to go on the *Holmes* Christmas programme. They did a segment on new dads, which included me and my son Levi, who had been born in August; former prime minister David Lange and his new daughter; and comedian Mark Hadlow and his new child.

David was in good form and grabbed Levi off me at one point, while telling me that his father, a doctor in South Auckland, delivered my father. I thought that was a cool thing to share with David, along with our children being the same age.

It was in the New Year of 1997 that I met journalist Liz Raizis, who, by chance, was at our house doing a documentary on Adele and her family's journey with breast cancer. She thought I should be doing radio for a job. Obviously, that was after seeing my face! She told me she had a very good contact at Newstalk ZB and that she would put a word in for me, which she did.

I wrote a radio show called 'Swinging the Billy' and took that, along with my guitar, to the interview where I met Bill Francis, the station's general manager. He wasn't a big man in stature, but he sure was a big man on radio.

I found Bill intimidating. There was good reason Newstalk ZB was number one in the country, and Bill had a fair bit to do with that. He told me to keep my billy-swinging show for now, but that he would give me a go on the overnight talkback programme.

Princess Diana had just died before I did my very first shift. I was terrible. I had barely even listened to any talkback, let alone run my own radio show - but I survived.

I went on to do fourteen years as a host: four and a half years on overnights at ZB, then I sat in the same seat as Barry had at Radio Pacific. I finished my hosting at Radio Live. I did enjoy my time on air.

Over the next few years, I got involved in a documentary or two about Barry. The filmmakers on one of these docos had only the dark side to report. Barry's ex-wives told their stories, but only the worst of what anyone said, including myself, made it on screen - there was no light and shade. They only wanted to show a brute, a violent one, which he certainly could be, but it wasn't all that he was.

I'd also been asked to be involved in a book called *The Search for the Great Kiwi Yarn*. The publisher had given me the task of contributing some yarns of my own. I'd never written before but gave it a go and wrote a number of short stories. Some made the final cut and were published. How about that?

But I was very conscious of following Barry. The storytelling and writing, they're too big shoes to fill, and in no way was this project about me trying to copy my father. I was simply enjoying myself.

Being on radio opened up a number of other opportunities for me. I was offered some TV work on a show called *How's Life?*, which I did for two years. It was fun while it lasted - I did enjoy working with everyone on that programme.

I had three wonderful trips overseas to incredible places with some of our audience from the radio. I toured the country twice with the 'Highway of Legends', a country music spectacular, after Gray Bartlett hired me to MC the tour. We played to 29,000 people on the first tour - a huge and resounding success.

Gray took me under his wing. He showed me how it all worked. He even got me singing and recording. Gray is a brilliant guitarist, promoter and entrepreneur, and also a great person to spend time with. He surrounded himself with great talent, like his good friend Brendan Dugan, Jodi Vaughan, the Hamilton County Bluegrass Band, a fantastic back-up band. After that, it was all promotion and fun. I learned so much and enjoyed every minute of it. I'm now slotting comfortably into the role of MC. Well, I mean, they are my initials.

I also toured the country with 'The Memories Roadshow'. We performed thirty-three shows in thirty-three towns and cities in eighteen months, and all the while I was doing my radio hosting. I was definitely keeping busy.

It was while working at Radio Pacific on a music show called 'Off the Record' that I met Roger Marbeck, who owned the iconic music store Marbecks in Queens Arcade. The show was on every Saturday night from 6 to 10pm, and to kick off the show every week I was joined by Roger for the first hour. He brought music from around the world in every week to discuss and promote on the programme. I got to know Roger over the next two years. He was so easy to talk to and a natural on air.

October 2007 was approaching - that was when I was to receive the copyright from Maggie and the courts. I knew I needed good people around me to help with this. I could think of no one better than Roger.

At the end of one of our Saturday nights on air together, I asked Roger if he would like to be involved with all things

Crump. He said he would be honoured. We shook hands. He has probably been cursing me ever since.

I knew I had just struck the golden ticket having Roger with me. He is still in charge of all things Crump today. No decision is made on any deal or contract without Roger's final sign-off.

'When we did finally receive the Crump copyright, it was generating very little. None of Barry's books were in print. We had to start from scratch.'

My friend Campbell Vance was now living in Australia. He is so self-motivated and always has been. He's very smart and, like a pit bull, he won't let go until he has the results he needs. I asked Campbell to join Roger and myself, and he accepted. I'm delighted to say Campbell is still working with us today as well, with the three of us directors of the company we named Bush Media.

When we did finally receive the Crump copyright, it was generating very little. None of Barry's books were in print. We had to start from scratch.

We had a chapter of a new Sam Cash novel Barry had started writing right before he passed away. He managed to complete only one chapter, but at least it was something. We also had some unfinished children's books in the Pungapeople series.

I decided to have a close look at the children's stories. It turns out that Barry had found a pair of children's shoes at Punakaiki, on the west coast of the South Island, and it gave him an idea for a children's book about the notorious Pungapeople, who could be incredibly naughty. The publisher partnered Barry up with the *Footrot Flats* illustrator, Murray Ball. Together, they put out *Mrs Windyflax and the Pungapeople* - it was a winner and sold well. The publisher wanted a series of Pungapeople tales, so Barry was asked to write six more. He completed four stories, all of which were published. There were the two remaining, but unfinished and not yet published, scripts in our hands. Barry had passed away before he could finish them.

It was then that I re-geared the formal arrangements for the family affairs. I contacted all my brothers, even those I hadn't yet met, and told them what I had done - that we were all now part of the Tall Trees Trust.

I looked over the two unfinished Pungapeople drafts. The first one was called *Professor Pingwit and the Pungapeople*. To get me in tune with the writing, I read the four books Barry had finished. There was definitely a rhythm to the writing that made for a great read. Barry had completed over half of the story for *Professor Pingwit and the Pungapeople*, and it didn't take very long before I had finished the text. It read and felt like Barry had written it himself.

Now, for the difficult part: we needed an illustrator. Murray Ball was unwell at that stage, and I didn't have a clue where else to go. By absolute chance, my children had heard me talking to my second wife, Jill, about this and suggested we use the lady who had just been to their school telling stories and drawing wonderful things. I contacted the school and got her details.

Her name was Lyn Kriegler - she is a fabulous illustrator, puppeteer and storyteller. She lived up in the Waitākere Ranges and I visited her. What talent and energy she had - I loved her work and asked for her help on *Professor Pingwit*. Lyn accepted on the spot and I left her the text.

She had many ideas of her own and added so much value to the project. She somehow included many of our family members' names in the book by painting them on buildings and businesses in the background of the story.

When the book was finished, it was wonderful - Lyn's illustrations and humour brought so much life to the story. We had Pungapeople puppets made for the official launch of the book and it went on to sell around 15,000 copies - a great success.

My time with Lyn did not finish there. We went on to visit and perform at many schools in greater Auckland, with Lyn encouraging me to write some children's stories of my own.

The sixth and last story in the series was called *Chief Awateri and the Pungapeople*. The writing was all over the place, with a totally different rhythm to the other stories in the series. It also had only eight stanzas that were usable, and we needed at least thirty-four. What Barry left in those eight stanzas was gold, but it was going to take a lot of figuring out to finish this one. It took even more time to complete than I anticipated, but the finished article is now something I'm quite proud of.

It was on a visit to the publisher that we found out how *Chief Awateri* was initially written. Barry had turned up drunk at the publishers, looking for money - something he had done more than once before. He was told he would have to produce some written work before they could pay him anything. So, he headed back to the pub and wrote *Chief Awateri and the Pungapeople* on bar coasters. He returned to the publishers with his unique manuscript, and they paid him. He then disappeared - I imagine back to the pub.

This would explain why the rhythm and text of the story was all over the place when we received it. Even then, there were some wonderful lines he'd managed to put together.

To date, this book has never been published. I still believe it's possibly the strongest story of the lot.

'He was told he would have to produce some written work before they could pay him anything. So, he headed back to the pub and wrote *Chief Awateri and the Pungapeople* on bar coasters.

Our inheritance as Barry's children is still a work in progress, but there is something else I've inherited from my father.

Barry died from a ruptured aneurysm in his main aorta. I went to the hospital with kidney stones two years ago, then thought no more of it. Next thing, I received a phone call from a surgeon who informed me that I have an aneurysm in exactly the same place as my father. At the time, I was also the same age as Barry when he passed away. I had to tell my brothers immediately so they could get themselves checked out. So far, so good - they are all clear.

Apparently, this aneurysm is hereditary. Mine is being monitored closely. I have no fear of this, and I hold no anger or resentment. It's only grown a little in size and I'm in very good hands.

LYALL In 1998, Colin Hogg was working on a documentary about Barry called *Crump: A Wandering Star*. He interviewed Mum, who looked and sounded great. When it was my turn they wired me up with a small microphone hidden under my shirt. I was plugged in, face powdered, lights, camera, and I was on.

'Lyall, did Barry ever beat you?' Colin asked.

The river of rage, a lion in a cage, a reason to resent.

I stood up, dragging the sound equipment off the table. I was crying, angry and wanted to hide away. I wanted to punch Colin. They unhitched me and I ran to my room, sobbing.

'Sorry, Lyall . . . I didn't mean to upset you. I should have shown you the questions. Sorry,' Colin said from behind the door. I just wanted to be left alone.

A few days later, I contacted the media company and insisted I redo the interview. I recited a heartfelt poem I'd written, spilled my guts. They only put in the bit where I told them Barry thought I was shallow and hollow like a log. I guess they agreed with him.

ERIK A few years after Barry's death, Mum and I went to visit his last wife, Maggie. It was only an hour's drive from where I lived, but it took us two attempts as we weren't sure of the address. Finally, we headed up a quiet road out of Tauranga and drove through rolling farmland until we reached the place.

It was a modest house, slightly run-down, with windows looking out over a neighbouring farm. Mum introduced me as one of Barry's sons.

'It was a peculiar feeling, knowing that Barry had sat on the couch I was sitting on now, but there was no connection here.'

Maggie was friendly enough but seemed tired. She asked about our lives and about her late husband's other sons. As we sat chatting, I looked around. It was a peculiar feeling, knowing that Barry had sat on the couch I was sitting on now, but there was no connection here.

After half an hour we left, and I've never been back.

MARTIN It was soon after receiving the copyright of Barry's works in 2007 that a man called Charlie contacted me. He asked to buy the movie option on Barry's book *Wild Pork and*

Watercress. We sat down at home together two or three times over a number of weeks to discuss Charlie's plans and how it would all work. I found out you buy the option, and this gives you the sole right to make the movie from the book. A typical option would run for two years, with the right of renewal.

Campbell Vance, my business associate, signed Charlie up. Charlie had quite an elaborate plan involving producers in Australia, millions of dollars and with Billy Connolly playing Uncle Hec. Two years went by and Charlie extended the option. We waited again until the option ran out. It was a waiting game - you need patience in the movie business, I found out.

It was 2009 when we decided to relaunch *A Good Keen Man* for the fiftieth anniversary of its first publication. We decided to tie this in with a reunion, bringing Barry's children together, with some of us meeting for the very first time.

Campbell had been hard at it and had arranged that the book would be stocked in all of the hunting and fishing stores. When finished, the book looked great with its new cover and size, with a fresh introduction by Barry's friend and mentor Kevin Ireland.

The publisher sent me on a nationwide book tour to meet and greet and promote it in stores everywhere. My brothers came from all different parts of the North Island, but one brother was unfortunately missing - Stephen. He was stuck in Australia and couldn't make it, though I did get to speak to him on the phone. The rest of us all met up though.

TV One were filming the moment we saw each other for the first time. This was followed by an interview. Ivan, who had always shunned the media, was brilliant in front of the camera. All of the brothers did so well.

I looked at us all together that day. We are all very different in personality and to look at, yet we all share this well-known father.

I got to know Erik a little better. He was handling this crazy day surprisingly well. He was calm under the spotlight, a natural. I had a good catch-up with Harry, who is now a very accomplished artist with his own gallery. I was so pleased he made it that day, especially given Stephen, his full brother, couldn't be there.

After all the media hype and activity, we met at Roger Marbeck's place and he put on a feast for us all. Lyall stayed the night at my place, and we had an excellent time with our youngest brother. I'd say that Lyall looks the most like Barry, and even shares some of his mannerisms.

Such a big effort was made by everyone involved.

It must have been about a year later when Harry called me to say that Stephen was back in the country. We all met up at Mount Maunganui, for a private reunion this time. It was so good to meet Stephen at last. The puzzle was now complete.

Campbell Vance had had several conversations with Taika Waititi, the film writer and director. Taika had been waiting in the wings for the previous option to be realised but got fed up waiting, so he went and made a movie of his own, *Boy*. He now wanted to take over the option on *Wild Pork and Watercress*, which had previously been licensed to Charlie. We were just happy to see some kind of movement.

Campbell set me up to meet Taika for a coffee in town. Taika's energy was infectious. He told me straight that movie-making had a different formula now - we didn't need all those millions - then laid out his plan.

We met several times over the next few months. It was at one of these meetings that Taika shared a little of the story of the relationship between him and his father - I've never forgotten it. That he spoke so openly and honestly about his father sealed the deal between us. I also met his producer, Carthew Neal. I had met Carthew before as he had filmed a programme with our family several years earlier. I was so pleased to see that he was going to be with us.

Taika was ready to take full control of the project. He knew exactly what he wanted to do with the book. He had already formed ideas in his mind. He just needed our signature to be let loose on the screenplay.

Taika told me the movie would be quite different from the book. The book had very little humour in it, which was unusual for Barry – the film, however, would have a great adventure with many laughs. I liked the idea of adding a few laughs to the story.

Taika also told me it might have coarse language in it, then surprised me when he asked what *I* would like to see in the movie. My reply was that Barry had brought to life a most unlikely bond and special friendship between a middle-aged, grumpy Pākehā bloke and a rebellious young Māori boy – somehow, he made this work on a page. If Taika could make that work on the screen, then we should have a winner on our hands. He could, and we did. Taika now had the green light.

There was a lot of positivity about Taika and about the movie. The industry started to buzz. We were treated so well by Taika and Carthew, and we were informed and included at nearly every stage of the shoot. Very generously, we were invited to watch the shooting of a few scenes.

Taika was excited when he talked about this young man he had been working with, Julian Dennison, who was to play the young Māori boy, Ricky. Taika really believed in him. The other news that delighted us all was the casting of Sam Neill as Uncle Hec. We were all starting to get excited.

After three months, the shooting of the film came to an end. Taika then took himself away overseas to do the editing for the movie, which he had named *Hunt for the Wilderpeople*.

The big release and highly anticipated New Zealand premiere of Taika Waititi's *Hunt for the Wilderpeople* arrived in March 2016. I brought along a large contingent of family and friends, including Uncle Colin. There were so many reporters, cameras, actors, actresses, all there for this most talked-about premiere. It was electric. I watched it with my daughter Olivia - she had already been on the film shoots with me, so she was also well involved in it all. We loved it. It was so much fun to watch a real Kiwi adventure be taken from a story in a book - Barry's book - onto the big screen.

I found Taika and hugged him. I told him how proud I was of both him and the movie. What an accomplishment! Even Uncle Colin was impressed.

'It was so much fun to watch a real Kiwi adventure be taken from a story in a book – Barry's book – to the big screen.'

As I was about to leave, I was confronted by Robin, Barry's ex-wife. She was very unhappy and vented about how she had been treated, and unloaded on me that she thought she was owed something. I told her she sounded like a victim and that she had to go, as this was not the time nor place to air grievances.

We both appeared in the paper the next morning. I was very annoyed at Robin using this time to grab attention, when I'd worked so hard and lost so much to get there. I also didn't want this spat to distract from the opening of the movie. When I think back now, I feel sad for Robin - she had every right to feel the way she did, after twelve difficult years with Barry. Hers was a natural reaction, in a way. She had been through so much and had lost so much herself. She was hurting. I hope time has helped her heal.

Hunt for the Wilderpeople was released worldwide to great fanfare - critics and the public alike loved the film, and it went on to become the highest-grossing New Zealand movie ever.

It was just wonderful to be a part of. I now think back to when Barry himself said that there had been some talk of turning one of his books into a movie. Well, Bazza, here it is - what do you reckon? I think he would have approved.

Within twelve months, we were invited to the New Zealand Film Awards. I took Olivia again. We had pre-drinks at a venue in town, where we sampled Sam Neill's own wine. It's a good drop. It was a thrill to talk to Sam. We were over the moon at his performance and absolutely chuffed to spend some time with him. At the awards, there was so much talk and excitement about Taika's movie and it won nearly every award on offer. It was amazing and heartening to see a New Zealand story do so well.

Barry holding baby Ivan
(with an unidentified child).

10.

The Kids Are All Right

Looking back, moving forwards

'We all have one thing in common: a father defined by his absence.'

IVAN I've used the Crump crap to my advantage and suffered the rest.

The sins of my father are well visited. I've been a drug addict from as soon as I could get my hands on them. I found cannabis at fourteen. At last, peace. When one desires to escape from oneself, it takes a lot of drugs, so that was the mission.

That progressed until I would have shot up food instead of eating it if that would have worked. So started a fifty-year romance with drugs.

The best thing about drugs is also the worst thing. You get a break from reality, a time out, but after a while that becomes your reality. After a few years, reality comes a-calling, and you have to deal with the past you wanted to avoid, plus the accumulated stuff you've acquired in the interim.

I've come off hard gear a few times. Every time was a chore, until the last time - that was enjoyable. I stopped because I wanted to, not because I should. My body woke up and so did my mind. My emotional body just exploded and I was unable to keep any sort of coherent balance. I shouldn't have been allowed out in public but, as usual, having no governing body, I went out and made a right royal cunt of myself again.

Still, no dead bodies, so who gives a shit?

ERIK When I had kids of my own, I threw myself into parenthood, determined that they would have the childhood I never did. It didn't quite work out that way, but they're good kids nonetheless. Two of them are off to university, so I can't have done too bad a job.

'I've encountered an endless procession of people throughout my life who had to tell me about the time they met Barry, had a drink with him, shared a yarn with him, or just saw him on the street.'

MARTIN There is no doubt that growing up the son of Barry Crump in the 1960s and '70s opened some doors, got me a job or two, and gave me opportunities perhaps others might not have had. There is also no doubt that most of the people I met didn't have the slightest interest in me personally. I just gave them some connection to the Good Keen Man himself; something they could tell their friends and family about.

I've encountered an endless procession of people throughout

my life who had to tell me about the time they met Barry, had a drink with him, shared a yarn with him, or just saw him on the street. I'd politely listen to it all.

I can tell you straight: Barry was never a father to me, but he did become a friend. As I see it now, I feel privileged to have had the time I did with Barry, but I never called him Dad. I reckon it would have felt wrong to the both of us anyway.

STEPHEN Jean, my biological mother, gave me Barry's older brother Bill's address, so I visited him in Tākaka.

I know now that Bill was often with Barry on his adventures, but was not mentioned - like with the crocodile hunting, getting marooned on Green Island, and the gold prospecting and mining.

I sorta got that Bill liked me, and I certainly liked him. He had a close relationship with Jack Daniels - the drink, not the bloke - so I would pick up a bottle or two duty-free whenever I visited him, and the yarns would start.

He was a ranger in the Abel Tasman National Park. He had a lovely home where every morning he would raise the Jack Daniels flag. Anyone wanting to find Bill's place was told to look out for the flag.

Home brew was another favourite of Bill's. I gather you're seeing a pattern here. Bill was a great storyteller, like his younger brother, and the alcohol oiled those wheels. I was envious of his lifestyle and location. I seemed to strike it lucky on my visits to him - I usually turned up on his days off.

Often, I would stay a few days. In that time, Bill would offer up bits of Barry to me - stories, their upbringing, moods and other insights. Most of our conversations, though, would lead back to Australia, as that was common ground for both of us.

IVAN My mum married a real good bloke, Wally Lester, who will always be my dad.

My family was anchored in my mother's love. Fierce, brave and loyal to the death. I was with her when she took her last breath. She was an awesome, giving woman to the end.

When she was dying, she told me that she lied to Barry and said she couldn't get pregnant as she knew he would shoot through, and she wanted to keep something from him.

Strange as it may seem, she hooked up with him again in later years. She reckoned the Barry she knew was gone and 'Crumpy' was all she found.

At one point, I was seriously thinking of changing my last name to Crumpson - the number of times I was introduced as 'Ivan, Barry Crump's son'.

I don't know how the others handled it. I felt annoyance, then attempted to be as graceful as I could be about it. Being the son of a man considered public property puts one in the same boat, so to speak. It's still happening.

He's been dead twenty-five years and, at sixty-three, I've largely come to terms with it. It still pisses me off sometimes, though. One has been automatically typecast, instead of being able to be wholly authentic; one is encouraged to behave in a certain fashion. It feels rude, but very forgivable. My response has been to (perhaps inappropriately) cock a snook at the whole thing.

Reflected popularity from an absentee parent that you haven't known is not particularly welcome. Though no one would know that. The ones who do know still do it, and I tend to just handle it well or badly, depending on my mood. It's made me avoid contact with people. I've become more distant and insular. That hasn't been too bad - I mostly like my own company.

I think the advantage of having grown up as the son of

Barry Crump was getting off traffic tickets and not getting arrested for assorted misdemeanours. People gave me a pass for aberrant behaviour. Jobs were more available and women were more interested.

I suppose, looking back, that it all made life more deluded. I carried a feeling of the need for real guidance, some curbing of my propensity for negative creation.

Barry and I both loved LSD, though there's nothing like it these days to compare. While dissimilarities were abundant as well, of course, we had a few things in common, as you can imagine. Lots of kids. He had the decency to bugger off and not show how much of a shit he was. I tried but, in retrospect, I probably shouldn't have bothered.

I've had sex with a lot of women, from all walks of life. Then the shallowness of my behaviour hit home, and that was the end of that. All that searching was a lot of fun - for all concerned, I hope - but unfulfilling. As far as I know, I've produced ten children; nine have survived. I'm very grateful to their mothers, who I blame entirely for my children being as cool as they are.

ERIK Family is a weird thing. Despite my unhappy childhood and the fact that I live half a country away, I still regularly visit my mum, brother and sister. None of us are super close, but we recognise that we're part of something bigger than ourselves. And yet, there's another family that I had barely thought of until a few years ago.

I always knew that, somewhere out there, there were other children of Barry Crump. At first, I heard that there were eleven of us, and then there were nine, but nobody seemed to know for sure. Then Martin got in touch, and I discovered that, in fact,

I had five brothers. I travelled up to Auckland to meet them for the first time.

It felt surreal to discover this sudden extended family of brothers, sisters-in-law, nephews and nieces. There were farmers and roading contractors, businessmen and artists, a ski guide and students - and all of them were supposed to be as much a part of my family as the brother and sister I had grown up with.

I've never been particularly gregarious, and I find social situations awkward at the best of times, but this felt doubly strange, like spending months travelling through the bush only to blunder into the midst of someone's birthday party.

We got on well enough, talking about our lives and the things we do. Everyone is so different and yet we all have one thing in common: a father defined by his absence.

We've stayed in touch, more or less. I attended Harry's wedding, and we've visited my other brothers a few times. But there seems to be something keeping us apart. Maybe it's just being caught up in our own lives, or a reluctance to pick at the scab of our childhood, I'm not sure. None of us had it easy. But my door is always open.

After a lifetime of thinking that my father had given me nothing, perhaps he's left me with something after all.

Over the years, my life settled into a pattern. I was successful in my career, eventually working for a series of internet start-ups that took me all over the world. I got married, had two children, divorced and remarried.

But I would still occasionally take out the photo Mum had given me and gaze at it. I had been about six when it was taken, and in the print there's a chubby-faced boy with unruly white-blond hair, looking proud to stand beside this giant of a man. We share the same dimple and, apparently, the same nose.

I would stare at that picture and wonder what might have been.

The answer, of course, is probably not much. Barry had wanted to have nothing to do with his offspring.

'It felt surreal to discover this sudden extended family of brothers, sisters-in-law, nephews and nieces.'

IVAN Barry told me more than a few lies to make me feel better about things. I didn't believe him, but I appreciated the effort. When one is as needy as I was, one listens for the truth.

I can't blame him for anything that I've done. He just didn't have any real influence, except to hurt and confuse me whenever I saw him when I was young. That may have influenced me to be distrustful of authority, I guess.

I think that, as a child, I just wanted my dad, and everybody else had more of him than I did, so resentment was my driving force. I'm envious of people who were lucky enough to spend more time with him than me, but I'm very grateful for knowing the guy as much as I did. I think it's not much fun to be in eye of the public as a collective animal. I suppose some enjoy it a lot, obviously.

ERIK The lack of a father stung sometimes. Around twenty years ago, I had to apply for a new birth certificate, and visited the Department of Internal Affairs in Wellington. I filled in the paperwork and waited for the copy to be made, but when the official came out, he asked me to follow him into a side room.

'I'm envious of people who were lucky enough to spend more time with him than me, but I'm very grateful for knowing the guy as much as I did.'

In hushed tones, he explained that there was something unusual about my birth certificate: my mother was listed, but there was just a blank space where my father's name should have been.

Another layer of paint over the old shell. I shouldn't have been surprised, I suppose.

Mum had said that Barry agreed not to deny I was his son, on the condition that she never asked him for money. He really had wanted nothing to do with me, or any of his children.

MARTIN Some of Barry's best gems, which would never be published, were in his letters to friends like Alex King - they were so witty and clever. This was the charmer at his best.

The Nugget of the Tattooed Leg
August 1994

Oh Kings!

An epistle has reached this outpost, brought to us by our faithful runners in a cleft stick, informing us of your safe return from the far-flung corners of the Kingdom. We hadn't heard from you since receiving the photograph of your travelling entourage and had consulted Sir Tuppeny O'Sullivan, the eminent Ngai Tahu Tohunga, and on his advice burnt a candle at both ends in support of our ardent prayers for your safe return. We rejoice to have you back with us.

There have been developments in the mystery surrounding the nugget of the tattooed leg. Ever since our acquisition of this dysphoric bauble we have suffered a series of terrible calamities.

Our great aunt Bertha, after a lifetime of pious chastity, has taken to prostitution and when last heard of had stowed away on a Russian trawler. My brother's wife, on being diagnosed as having Mad Cow Disease, ran away to Surfers Paradise with the neighbour's Hereford bull. My other brother's eleven year old daughter got hold of his credit card and poured the whole family fortune into the pokey machine at the Arthurs Point pub. My brother-in-law has become schizophrenic and the last report we had of him was that he'd paid his income tax twice. Maggie has taken up Transcendental meditation and sits cross-legged for many hours each day on the top of Mount Barker, meditating on the various philosophies and religions of the world, whilst engaging in ecstatic contemplation of her navel. I think she's become introverted. And now my dog is acting strange.

It's all become too much of a burden for me and I can no longer keep the secret of the accursed nugget of the tattooed leg to myself. Accordingly I reveal its origin to your eminences. The truth is enshrined in the enclosed booklet. I trust you will treat the information therein with discretion, in the interests of maintaining harmony and order in the Realm.

Inexpressibly Unburdened,
I remain, Your Humble And Obedient Servant,
John B Cramp, Esquire,
Barker Station,
Otago.

(Love, Barry and Maggie)

When I was spending time with him once, he said he had to go away for a while.

'If I don't get this written down, it'll be lost.'

So he headed off to the Mackenzie Country. He got himself a job as a cook on a high-country sheep station and was gone for a few months. Out of this came the story *Bullock Creek* – not a huge seller by any means, but it captured the life of high-country sheep-herding of the past. He had felt a need to record this for us all.

It's in stories like this that I truly believe Barry was doing a service to all New Zealanders.

I am proud of my father - for the mark he has left behind, for telling us about ourselves in a language we all understood. He definitely made us laugh and entertained us all; and somehow we recognise someone we know in the characters he created.

As for the dark side of Barry, I'm very sorry for those who he hurt physically and emotionally, especially his wives and partners, who endured more than most.

IVAN Barry truly was a naturally charming man in many ways and would often get away with doing and saying things that were quite inappropriate.

He'd walk down after doing a speech or whatever, pick a woman out of the audience and take her for the night.

Charisma to burn, that lad. People got jealous and bad-mouthed him occasionally, but these negative-vibe merchants wouldn't know if their arse was on fire. (I went through a phase of saying that a lot, until one day I was welding the exhaust on my bulldozer when hot metal ignited the oil and twigs in the belly pan, and I was standing there with flames around my arse, too engrossed in the job to notice. My kids were just watching, until it became noticeable to me. They all reckoned I wouldn't know if my arse was on fire, and they were right.)

My philosophy is if I'm not living on the edge, I'm taking up too much room. Part of my frenetic lifestyle back then was to risk it all - explosives, fast bikes, cars, taking a lot of drugs and, of course, promiscuity.

Though married to an extremely beautiful woman with everything plus, the constraints of the situation were too much for me. None were put on me, I just felt it. I've been more amoral than immoral.

One thing I will always regret, though, is that I wasn't able to show or live my better nature with my children. I've been unable to be a good dad, to my deepest shame. While I have been good company most of the time, when it comes to my children, I have fallen down.

I've been a very lucky chap - I've already lived much longer than expected. My family didn't think I'd make it to twenty, given I flirted with death continually.

I'm very grateful for everything I've got right now. Totally undeservedly, I've found love again and I'm sincerely happy . . . go figure.

STEPHEN As I've got to know myself better, I have wondered what traits I might have taken on from Barry, but I reckon I have more of my mum Jean in me, as I'm shy and a people-pleaser. I couldn't for a minute comprehend doing some of the things Barry did - radio, TV, acting. I could never do that.

I've also never hunted or shot a gun, but I have done some tramping and I do enjoy the outdoors. I'm a jack of all trades and can turn my hand to many things. I'm your fix-it guy - definitely no academic.

The only thing I can think of that I might have been a bit better than him at is being a father, but even then, I'm not condemning him. He lived in an era when a lot of dads were absent, but because he was famous and living in something like a fishbowl, he copped it from all sides.

When I read *In Endless Fear*, by Barry's younger brother Colin, it told me volumes about why Barry so struggled to be a dad. And if I want to know any more about Barry, I can always pick up a book and read about him, because so much has been written, which makes me luckier than some. So many don't get anything like that when it comes to their parents.

'If I want to know any more about Barry, I can always pick up a book and read about him.'

HARRY In my recollections, I've left out a lot and chosen to recount the early times only. The early times are more harmless for me to talk about, considering other family, other pain and circumstance.

My memories are colourful and hurtful.

My father endured a lot, not just from my grandfather, as is well recorded, but from the passivity of his mother.

I met them on one occasion and felt an overwhelming indifference. I thought, *What are you both doing here?* Though only eighteen years old at the time, I knew neither of them had properly cared for my father. Fuck them.

None of my brothers have abused their children. We might make mistakes - everyone does - but hats off to a better world.

LYALL It dawned on me when I met my other brothers, Barry's sons, that we are all sensitive beings with our own unique stories. I've got to know my other brothers and some of their kids. I didn't help Martin with the court case but agreed with what he was doing.

I give ultimate respect to Mum. I love her and my new dad, and my bros, and all the people I know and knew; and I loved my old dad, old Barry, and his wide world that opened me up to so much.

I hold no grudge against anyone. Quite the opposite. I'm grateful to all the people I've encountered throughout my life.

In the end, all that is left is love and its wonderful shadows. I married an amazing woman and got to know her beautiful family. We've had a marvellous girl who has a lot of Barry's better traits.

To the chagrin of Dad, I kept the Crump name and still have a pride in my famously flawed father who brought me into this amazing world of dreams.

MARTIN Over the years, I have collected music, recordings, photos, stories, interviews, articles and film about Barry. There is one thing he told me, not written or recorded anywhere that I have seen, but it has always stuck with me. He simply said: 'If all's to be all okay, your kids have to be better than you.'

That'll do me.

Photo Credits

CS = colour section

Martin Crump collection: 6, 12, 17, 18, 26, 30, 32, 76, 96, 105, 108, 112, 116, 129, 134, 150, 156, 158, 160, 164, 168, 174, 178, 180, 184, 186, 189, 202, 220; CS4, CS5

Vanda Lynden collection: 22, 36, 39, 42, 44, 48, 68, 89, 100, 171; CS1, CS2, CS3

Alamy: 125

***New Zealand Herald* archive:** 176; CS6

Stuff Limited: CS7, CS8

Barry Crump Bibliography

– By Barry Crump

A Good Keen Man (1960)
Hang on a Minute Mate (1961)
One of Us (1962)
There and Back (1963)
Gulf (1964)
Scrapwagon (1965)
The Odd Spot of Bother (1967)
Warm Beer and Other Stories (1969)
A Good Keen Girl (1970)
No Reference Intended (1971)
Bastards I Have Met (1971)
Fred (1972)
Shorty (1980)
Puha Road (1982)
The Adventures of Sam Cash (1985)
Wild Pork and Watercress (1986)
Barry Crump's Bedtime Yarns (1988)
Bullock Creek (1989)
The Life and Times of a Good Keen Man (1992)
Gold and Greenstone (1993)
Arty and the Fox (1994)
Forty Yarns and a Song (1995)
Mrs Windyflax and the Pungapeople (1995)
Crumpy's Campfire Companion (1996)
As the Saying Goes (1996)
Song of a Drifter (1996)
Back Down the Track (1998)
The Pungapeople of Ninety Mile Beach (1999)
Harry Hobnail and the Pungapeople (2002)
Mr Tanglewood and the Pungapeople (2005)
Professor Pingwit and the Pungapeople (2009)

– About Barry Crump

Barry Crump: A Tribute to Crumpy, 1935–1996, various authors (1996)
The Old Dynamite Shack: Crump – The Untold Stories, George Johnston (1999)
A Life in Loose Strides: The Story of Barry Crump, Colin Hogg (2000)
The Hermit of Cemetery Island, George Johnston (2002)
In Endless Fear: A True Story, Colin Crump (2002)
In Salting the Gravy: A Tale of a Twelve-year Marriage to Barry Crump, Robin Lee-Robinson (2004)

When Social Welfare threatens to put Ricky into care, the overweight Māori boy and cantankerous Uncle Hec flee into the remote and rugged Urewera. The impassable bush serves up perilous adventures, forcing the pair of misfits to use all their skills to survive hunger, wild pigs and the vagaries of the weather. Worse still are the authorities, determined to bring Ricky and Uncle Hec to justice. But despite the difficulties of life on the run, a bond of trust and love blossoms between the world-weary man and his withdrawn sidekick.

This rattling good yarn has been made into a major movie: *Hunt For the Wilderpeople*, directed and written by Taika Waititi, and starring Sam Neill and Julian Dennison.

Also available as an ebook.